Muskegon Seventh-day Adventist School

# Contributions of Women

# EDUCATION

by Mary W. Burgess

Dillon Press, Inc.
Minneapolis, Minnesota

Library of Congress Cataloging in Publication Data

Burgess, Mary W.
　Contributions of women: education.

Bibliography: p. 142
　SUMMARY: Brief biographies of six influential women in the field of education: Emma Hart Willard, Mary Lyon, Martha Berry, Patty Smith Hill, Florence Sabin, Mary McLeod Bethune.
　1. Educators—United States—Biography—Juvenile literature. [1. Educators—Biography. 2. Women—Biography] I. Title. II. Title: Education.
LA2311.B87　　　　370'.92'2 [B] [920]　　　　74-32070
ISBN 0-87518-080-9

Designed by Pat Jerina

©1975 by Dillon Press, Inc. All rights reserved
Second printing 1977

Dillon Press, Inc., 500 South Third Street
Minneapolis, Minnesota 55415

Printed in the United States of America

# Contents

INTRODUCTION ........................ 5

A PLAN THAT WORKED ............... 7
   EMMA HART WILLARD (1787-1870): Early advocate of education for women

A NOBLE SCHOOL ..................... 29
   MARY LYON (1797-1849): Founder of Mount Holyoke College

NOBODY DARED SAY NO .............. 47
   MARTHA BERRY (1866-1942): Educator in the Appalachian Mountains

"CHECKERBOARD" TEACHING ......... 71
   PATTY SMITH HILL (1868-1946): Pioneer of the modern kindergarten

PASSING IT ON ....................... 87
   FLORENCE SABIN (1871-1953): Teacher of medical science, crusader for public health

I LEAVE YOU LOVE ................... 111
   MARY McLEOD BETHUNE (1875-1955): Tireless worker for education of black Americans

OTHER OUTSTANDING WOMEN ........ 135

SUGGESTED READING ................. 142

The photographs are reproduced through the courtesy of Emma Willard School, Mount Holyoke College Library, Berry College, Association for Childhood Education International, Johns Hopkins University, Bethune-Cookman Institute, and Alva Museum Replicas, Inc.

# Introduction

From pioneer times until today, early childhood education has been primarily in the hands of women. And until quite recently, one of the few professions recognized as suitable for women has been that of teaching.

Yet the women written about in this book were forced to overcome great obstacles in order to blaze new trails in the world of education: Emma Willard, to show that girls could and should learn mathematics and sciences as well as boys; Mary Lyon, to continue the education of young women through the college level and in a publicly supported institution; Martha Berry, to bring education to the poor children of the Appalachian mountains; Patty Smith Hill, to release the springs of creativity in the minds of kindergarten children; Florence Sabin, to demonstrate that women could teach at the highest level of education; and Mary McLeod Bethune, to give black girls a chance to learn to read and write.

Each of these women was forced to make great personal sacrifices to achieve her goal, yet each refused to believe that the task was impossible. Have faith in yourself, they seem to tell us, then work, work, work.

The stories told here suggest that perhaps all of us should follow our special dream. Dreams can change the world.

*Emma Willard, founder of the Emma Willard School, was the first woman in the United States to actively support higher education for women.*

# A Plan That Worked

## EMMA HART WILLARD

*Early advocate of education for women.*

"Emma! Emma . . a . . aa!"

Mistress Hart's voice carried clearly across the yard, but Emma pretended not to hear. The next call, however, contained a warning note that she did not dare to ignore.

"Emma Hart! Come here this instant!"

Hastily, Emma slid down the trunk of the backyard maple and ran to the kitchen door.

"Here I am, Mother," she said. "Look what I just found: three baby robins in their nest, and a fourth just breaking out of his little blue shell! See — over there?" And she waved her hand toward the leafy maple.

But her mother was not easily distracted. "You should have been in the house half an hour ago, working on your sampler. You know you must have it done when you start school at the end of the week."

"Yes, but I hate sewing," complained Emma. Then quickly she added, "I'll do it, Mother. Right now. And you'll have nothing to be ashamed of when I finish."

Emma went into the large keeping room, or kitchen, where most of the family's living took place. Her father, Captain Samuel Hart, was the owner of a prosperous farm in Berlin, Connecticut, where Emma had been born on February 23, 1787. She was the next to the youngest of sixteen children.

Seating herself on a bench under a window, Emma pulled out her sampler and began to cross-stitch the tulips and daisies which decorated the outside border. Resentfully punching the needle in and out of the homespun linen, she repeated the verse in the center of the design:

> If I Am Right, Oh, Teach My Heart
> Still In The Right To Stay.
> If I Am Wrong, Thy Grace Impart
> To Find The Better Way.

"Why doesn't somebody find a better way to educate girls?" she said to herself. "Boys have everything their way — at least they don't have to do this sewing!"

Emma wove the needle back and forth for an hour, then stuffed the linen back into the sewing box and darted outside.

"That one! Whatever are we to do with her!" sighed her mother. "Always out wandering in the woods, climbing trees, pestering her brothers to go hunting with them. Pray God that she will change her ways in time."

True to her promise, ten-year-old Emma finished her sampler just before the district school opened in June. But she left for school without much enthusiasm. It wasn't that she didn't like studying, but she wanted to study something more than Dilworth's speller and the Psalter and the catechism. If only the teacher would allow her to use one of the boys' books for reading, she thought, it would make school much more interesting.

Connecticut was the only New England state at this time to provide public grammar schools for its young people. These were the district schools like the one Emma attended. At first, girls were allowed to attend only in summer, when the boys were busy with farming. And girls were expected to learn only the minimum of the three Rs. These distinctions Emma found very annoying.

One night Emma decided to bring up the subject of her schooling with her father. "Father, would you like me to read to you tonight?"

"Why, of course," responded Captain Hart. "Did you copy something in school that interested you?"

"Not in that old school! The teacher treats us like a class of stupids, able to do little more than copy letters on our slate."

Mimicking the high monotone of a bored student, she began to quote a lesson from her speller:

> She fed the old hen; the hen was fed by her.
> I met him in the lot. The cow was in the lot.
> See how hot the sun is. It is hot today.
> See the dog run to me.
> She has a new hat. She put her hat on the bed.
> Did you get my hat? I did not get the hat.

Her father could not resist smiling. He patted Emma on the arm. "There, now, lass, he means well, I'm sure. What are you going to read for me, then, if it isn't a lesson from school?"

"It's from one of your own books," said Emma.

## 10 A Plan That Worked

"Close your eyes and see if you can guess it."

Obediently Captain Hart closed his eyes as Emma began to read:

> Come, and trip it as ye go
> On the light fantastic toe.
> And in thy right hand lead with thee,
> The mountain nymph, sweet Liberty.

When she had finished, her father beamed with pride. "Well spoken, little lass! John Milton himself would be happy with your reading. And your mother too, I'll warrant."

Mrs. Hart glanced up briefly from her loom, but murmured only, "So that is what she has been doing while the hems went unmended and the garden unweeded."

Emma realized her advantage and plunged immediately into her argument: "You see, Father, I can learn just as well as any boy. Yet girls are allowed to go to school only in the summer. Father, please let me go along with my brothers when the winter school opens. You are on the school committee; I know you can arrange it!"

Captain Hart puffed steadily on his corncob pipe.

"We'll see, we'll see," was his only reply. "Time for bed, now."

Both parents watched Emma go up the rough stairway to the second floor.

"It will be a problem to handle that one," sighed the captain. "She has a real head on her shoulders."

Upstairs, Emma waited until her parents had gone to bed and all the lights were out. Then she relighted her candle and began once more to read. When the words began to blur, she blew out her candle and floated off into a dreamland filled with dozens of schoolrooms, each of which contained a single teacher and a single pupil — herself!

Throughout the summer, Captain Hart helped Emma with both her reading and her spelling. Also under his instruction, she learned to draw circles, squares, and triangles on the hearth, absorbing simple rules of geometry as she traced the lines with her charcoal pencil.

It had long been the captain's custom to read to his family as they gathered around the fireplace during the evenings. His favorites were *Paradise Lost* and *The Spectator*. Emma's eager attention pleased him and at last he agreed that she should attend the winter school.

Emma was determined to prove herself as she marched off to school one sunny autumn morning. Seating herself on one of the small benches reserved for the younger children, she glanced about the room. No blackboards, globes, or maps adorned the simple schoolroom, but Captain Hart had supplied his daughter with some unruled paper. Homemade ink filled the pewter inkstand. The teacher, who had been hired partly for his quill-making ability, shaped quills and ruled copypaper for his young students while he listened to them read.

When Emma heard her name called, she slid quickly off the bench, curtsying politely as was the custom, and presented her copybook to the teacher. Without a word he accepted it, nodded dismissal, and called the older children up to read. They formed a half-circle in front of him and began reading a verse each from the Old Testament.

"The Earth is the Lord's and the fullness thereof," intoned Jacob Bingham.

"I can read as well as that," thought Emma to herself. Accepting her copybook from the master's outstretched hand, she quickly copied the alphabet he had printed and returned the book. He did not interrupt the reader, who was stumbling over a paragraph of Hebrew names, but raised his eyebrows as he glanced at Emma's work. He wrote a longer set of sentences and handed back her book.

Emma glanced in happy surprise at the exercise. It was the beginning sentences of a fable in Webster's blueback speller; she had heard her brother read it many times.

> An old man found a rude boy upon one of his trees stealing apples, and desired him to come down; but the young saucebox told him plainly he would not.
>
> "Won't you?" said the old man. "Then I will fetch you down." So he pulled up some turf or grass and threw it at him; but this only made the youngster laugh, to think the old man should pretend to beat him down from the tree with grass only.

Here the teacher's copy ended, but Emma continued writing the story from memory:

> "Well, well," said the old man, "if neither words nor grass will do, I must try what virtue there is in stone." So the old man pelted him heartily with stones, which soon made the young chap hasten down from the tree and beg the old man's pardon.
>
> MORAL: If good words and gentle means will not reclaim the wicked, they must be dealt with in a more severe manner.

The next day Emma was allowed to read with the oldest boys. But she became more and more impatient about her schooling. Her main complaint was that the teachers never talked about the meaning of anything. All the students did was memorize, recite, and spell. Of what use was that, she felt, if they never learned to think for themselves?

After she completed the course at the district school, she entered an academy which had recently opened in a nearby village. This school welcomed girls as well as boys. There, for two years, in 1802 and 1803, Emma enjoyed the advantages of a school run by a Yale graduate named Dr. Thomas Miner. His teaching was quite different from what Emma had known before. Dr. Miner encouraged her in her studies and helped stimulate her to think. To his criticisms of her compositions, she would reply in witty rhymes, and thus began her lifelong interest in the writing of poetry.

At the end of her second term under Dr. Miner, she applied for a teacher's position at her old district school and was accepted. She was seventeen years old then, a pretty girl with blue eyes, fair hair, and high coloring. And her head was filled with ideas for improving the teaching of young children. She was determined to follow Dr. Miner's example. Her students would not just memorize and recite; they would learn how to think for themselves.

It was the opening day of school. Emma had risen early, carefully piled her long hair on top of her head to make herself look older, and rearranged her school notes half a dozen times. She sat rigidly in her chair as she nervously picked at her breakfast. Her sisters teased her about the problems she was going to have trying to discipline the older boys, many of them bigger than herself, and she could feel her knees beginning to shake under the table. Then it was time to set out.

At precisely nine o'clock, Emma rang the large brass school bell. Eyeing her curiously, the children trooped in. As she called each one to her desk to examine him or her for assignment to a grade, the class became more and more noisy. A passing carriage aroused the curiosity of the boys, two of whom jumped out of the open window in pursuit, returning leisurely to their studies half an hour later.

Meanwhile, the hubbub increased.

"Children! You must be quiet! How can you expect to learn anything?"

Her pleas were ignored.

A moment later, a bloodcurdling shriek brought the teacher to her feet. She saw a seven-year-old girl running toward her, blue ink dripping down her sparkling white pinafore.

"Douglas has ruined my new dress!" wailed the child.

Emma put her arm around the girl, consoling her and helping clean up the stain. Then she had Douglas stand in the corner until noon. But the commotion continued, and the morning wore away slowly. When twelve o'clock finally arrived, Emma was in a state of exhaustion and panic.

Dismissing the class, she hurried to the other classroom, wailing to her fellow teacher, "Mrs. Peck, I can't control them at all. I have appealed to their sense of fair play, their parents' ambitions for them, their common sense — nothing works."

"And nothing will work," responded Mrs. Peck calmly, "nothing will work in the beginning except severe discipline."

"I cannot," answered Emma. "I never struck a child in my life."

"It is the only way," said her friend, "and you must do it."

When the noisy children filed into the classroom after lunch, they saw five green rods on Miss Hart's desk. Emma explained to them that the rods would be used to discipline any student who broke a rule.

After a short while, a boy named Charles rose from his seat and began walking casually toward the door. Emma grabbed one of the rods, seized the boy by his arm, and gave him several good whacks. Then, still gripping his arm, she led him back to his seat and plopped him into it with some force.

For a time, quiet prevailed. Then two of the boys climbed up on their benches to look out the window. When they ignored her command to take their seats, each of them received the same treatment as Charles. By the end of the day Emma had broken all five rods. But she had made her point. When school began the following morning, the young teacher laid a dozen more switches across her desk before calling the class to order. Never again did she have to apply the rod.

As a teacher, Emma was quick to praise students for effort and accomplishment, but she demanded cooperation and daily study. Complimenting the parents on their children's work from time to time gained parental support as well. By and large, the term proved very rewarding, and Emma was certain that she had found her calling.

That winter, Emma went back to school herself. At Misses Pattens' school in Hartford, she improved her skills in teaching reading and arithmetic, and she learned lace and embroidery work as well. The next summer she helped earn her school expenses by teaching a group of students in the Hart farmhouse. Then she was selected to head the Berlin academy, the same school she had attended under Dr. Miner. Here she began the custom of holding public examinations of her students. The parents enjoyed the event, and the students were motivated to concentrate on their studies.

Since school terms lasted only a few months, Emma found time between sessions to continue her own education in Hartford. The school curriculum included geography, French, painting and drawing, and dancing. Each new subject stimulated her alert mind. She especially enjoyed the dancing, and she discovered that it lent vigor to her body and her mind.

The owner of the house where she boarded in Hartford was a man who read widely in politics and philosophy. Emma enjoyed many interesting conversations with him. One day they were discussing the merits of Noah Webster's spelling book, then in general use in New England schools, as opposed to the older Dilworth speller. Her landlord excused himself for a moment, returning with a current issue of the Boston *Post*.

"Listen to what your beloved Dr. Webster has to say about female education," he remarked with a twinkle in his eye. And he read, " 'Its object should be what is useful — English, geography, history. Young ladies should not see the vicious part of mankind.' "

Emma spoke up at once.

"Dr. Webster has been so busy with his dictionary and his blueback speller that he has given little thought to the role of women in the development of our nation. Only men who have had the advantage of early training by educated women are likely to be successful in public life. And fortunately, my dear doctor, there are other views on the subject." And she brought him some of her own reading material. "Let me read you what Benjamin Rush, the famous Philadelphia doctor, has to say."

> Instrumental music, French, drawing are a great waste of time. How many useful ideas might be picked up in these hours from history, philosophy, poetry, and the numerous moral essays with which our language abounds. Let the ladies of a country be educated properly, and they will not only make and administer its laws, but form its manners and character. . . . The influence of female education would be still more extensive and useful in domestic life.

Soon Emma found herself more and more committed to increasing the educational advantages of young women. At the same time, her reputation as an excellent teacher was spreading into other New England states. When a position was offered her as head of a girls' academy in Middlebury, Vermont, she accepted. Emma was then just twenty years old.

Middlebury was quite a city for those times. It had sawmills and grist mills on its Otter Creek, and marble quarries as well. Middlebury College, founded in 1800, gave an air of culture to the town and assured a high interest in education. The academy for girls was one of the first in New England. It had closed for a few years but now Emma had been hired to reopen it. The task was by no means an easy one. She wrote home in August, 1807:

"Dear Mama, I go to school generally before nine, and stay till one; come home, snatch my dinner, go again, and stay till almost sundown; come home, and dress in a great hurry to go abroad; get home about ten, fatigued enough to go to bed and lie till seven the next morning, with hardly time enough to mend my stockings."

New England winters can be cold and unpleasant. Emma had to walk from her boarding house to the academy, and her classes were in a large, long room, with only an open fire for warmth. To combat the chill, she introduced dancing, having the class sing while they worked out the steps on the cold floor. So successful did this effort prove, both in increased enthusiasm and in improved health, that afterwards Emma included it in every curriculum she taught.

After she had been at the Middlebury academy for less than five years, romance interrupted Emma's career. John Willard, a widower who was a physician and an influential political figure in Vermont, began calling on Emma. She was attracted by his good manners, his intelligence, and especially by his willingness to show respect for her own intelligence. They were married in 1809 and a year later a son John was born. Emma settled down into the new job, for her, of being a wife and mother.

Soon her husband's nephew John came to board with them while he attended Middlebury College. John's coming was a fortunate event. He was a friendly, scholarly young man, delighted to be a part of the Willard household. Emma listened eagerly to accounts of his college life. Reading his textbooks and listening to descriptions of his classes, she once more became sharply aware of the great differences between male and female education. Women simply did not have the opportunity for advanced study, as men did.

She decided to take up the study of geometry

again. Later, she asked her young nephew to give her a thorough examination in the subject. He did so, and assured her that she knew as much as any student in his class. Her appetite for learning sharpened once again and she began studying Palwy's *Moral Philosophy* and Locke's *Essay Concerning Human Understanding*.

"The female mind is just as capable of education as that of a male," she told her husband. "It is not fair that women are denied the pure joy of learning."

"Look out, Emma; you'll bring down a peck of troubles on your head if you mention that idea in public," warned Dr. Willard, although he sympathized with her point of view. "Women are not supposed to hold opinions on serious subjects."

"Well, I do, and I plan to continue to study!"

A few years later the good doctor had reason to be glad that his young wife had resumed her education. The Vermont State Bank, of which Dr. Willard was a director, was robbed, and its directors were called upon to make up the loss. Dr. Willard mortgaged all his property, leaving little for everyday expenses. To increase their income, Emma Willard turned naturally to the familiar schoolroom, and she decided to start a new school for girls of high school age. The War of 1812 was moving into its final stages and her son was three and a half years old when she opened her school in the spring of 1814. It was immediately successful, with thirty day students and forty more who boarded in the Willard home.

"I spent from ten to twelve hours a day teaching," she later wrote. "On extraordinary occasions, as preparing for examination, fifteen hours; besides always having under investigation some one new subject which, as I studied, I simultaneously taught to a class of my ablest pupils. Hence, every new term some new study was introduced; and, in all their studies, my pupils were very thoroughly trained. . . . My first duty as teacher required of me to make my pupils, by explanation and illustration, *understand* their subject. . . . Then, in the second stage, I made each scholar recite, in order that she might remember. . . . Then the third process was to make the pupil capable of communication."

Emma was delighted at the chance to try out ideas she had been considering for many years. She was certain that girls could learn as well as boys. Beginning with the standard curriculum for girls, she gradually introduced more difficult subjects, one at a time. As she discovered how much her girls could achieve, her anger at the discrimination practiced against her sex grew.

"Legislators can spend thousands of dollars for the education of boys, but when was anything ever done by the public to promote education for girls?" she would ask over and over again.

She began to work out a specific plan for educating girls, hoping to convince the public and thus lawmakers that state funds should be appropriated to support the proposal. Not daring to call it a college, she named her proposed school a Female Seminary, and she wrote up her ideas in a *Plan for Improving Female Education,* as she called it. She submitted a copy of the manuscript to New York's Governor DeWitt Clinton, who supported the idea of educating women. He was impressed, and he urged the legislature to make some provision for the improvement of female education. In 1818 Dr. Willard accompanied his wife to Albany, where they lobbied for the plan among the New York legislators, trying to convince them of its importance. But the legislature refused to appropriate any money for the school, only granting it a charter. The name of the school was the Waterford Academy for Young Ladies. By this time Emma had decided to move her school to Waterford, New York, at the town's invitation and promise of support.

Convinced that the ideas in her plan were both sound and useful, Emma published it at her own expense. The resulting book had four main parts: (1) Defects in the current system of education for girls; (2) General principles for regulating education; (3) A detailed plan for running a female seminary; and (4) Benefits that would result from this kind of seminary. The plan emphasized the absolute necessity of having state support of these schools. It was widely read and discussed in both the United States and Europe. Emma's reputation as a crusader for female education continued to grow.

In the fall of 1819, she opened the Waterford school with twenty-two boarding students and a staff of Willard-trained teachers. She herself taught mathematics. When some of her students successfully passed a public examination in the subject, a few men finally acknowledged that it was indeed possible for a woman to understand the subject.

"And that is only the beginning, girls!" she beamed with enthusiasm. "We can learn anything they can!"

Dr. Willard was Emma's business manager. One morning she announced with excitement that Governor Clinton had again asked the legislature to appropriate money for the Waterford school. Both she and her husband were confident that this time they would be granted the money, for they felt that the public was now behind their efforts.

And the state senate, indeed, did appropriate two thousand dollars for Emma Willard's school, but the measure failed to pass the house. The Willards were very disappointed. How could they continue to operate, they wondered. What could they do?

At that very time, however, a committee of leading citizens from Troy, New York, invited the well-known Mrs. Willard to open a school in their town. They promised to furnish a building for her school and to appoint a group of women to help adapt the building to her requirements. The Willards were thrilled.

"We don't want to leave your town," they explained tactfully to their Waterford supporters. "But our lease expires in May and the town has no plans to renew it. We have no alternative."

So in 1821 they moved to Troy. Even though Emma was the founder and director of the school, the lease for the building had to be signed by Dr. Willard; a married woman could not legally sign a lease.

When the Troy Female Seminary opened in September, ninety girls from seven states were enrolled. Emma Hart Willard was a happy woman. Only thirty-four years old, she was already seeing her dream come true. A real education for girls was now to be possible.

Immediately she put her plan into execution. A typical day began at 7:00, or at 6:30 in summer. Thirty minutes' study, thirty minutes' exercise, then breakfast. Classes or study until noon, when the main meal was served. When the afternoon classes ended at four, a free period was given until the 6:30 supper. Afterward an hour of dancing was scheduled, then more study till bedtime. Emma gave regular lectures, encouraging good manners and a neat appearance. Church attendance, daily Bible reading, and prayers were taken for granted.

The girls at Troy Seminary were assigned in pairs to small rooms for study and sleep. The furnishings consisted of a double bed, bureau, two chairs, and a small wood stove. Water, of course, had to be fetched from the yard pump; a pan of coals was kept in the hall to light fires with. Student monitors were alert for signs of bad housekeeping, such as a wrinkled or cluttered bed, or gloves carelessly left on a chair. After a girl got a certain number of demerits, she had to go see Mrs. Willard in her office. Usually, a little talk proved discipline enough.

How busy Emma was! Of course, one of the

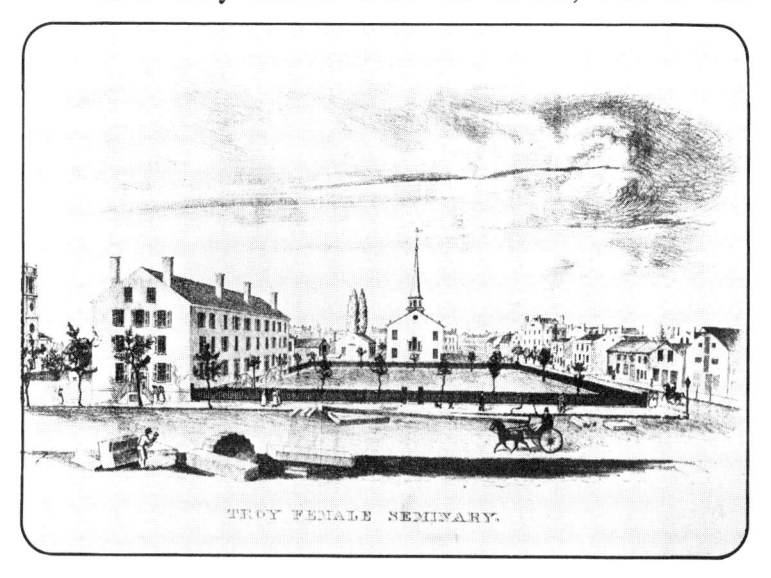

*The original buildings of the Troy Female Seminary*

most important things was the curriculum. Advanced courses in history and natural philosophy (physics) were included, then modern languages, painting, and music. Increasingly sure of her teaching techniques, Emma began work on a geography textbook. The textbooks then available were usually dull and boring, with page after page of facts to be memorized. Emma wrote her book keeping in mind that students needed to learn how to think. Her textbook even used maps and charts to show the interrelationships of countries. She was co-author of the volume finally published in 1823: *A System of Universal Geography on the Principles of Comparison and Classification.* It achieved instant success and was soon used in schools throughout the United States, contributing to Emma's widening reputation. Emma was invited to submit an article to the *Literary Magazine* of New York on the subject, "Will Scientific Education Make Woman Lose Her Dependence on Man?"

"If you're an example, it certainly will!" teased her husband. Dr. Willard recognized the importance of his wife's ambitions and continued to serve as her aide and enthusiastic supporter. Their married life was very happy, and when he later died, in 1825, she felt the loss deeply.

The Troy Seminary became more and more famous, and Troy graduates were in great demand as teachers. Visits from dignitaries became a regular occurrence at the school. The size of the campus was increased, and more buildings were added.

The visit to the seminary in 1824 of General Lafayette, the Revolutionary War hero, was a memorable occasion. The young women had covered an arch over the doorway with evergreens and flowers. It bore this message: "We owe our schools to freedom; freedom to Lafayette." Mrs. Willard had composed a song for the occasion, and two young girls presented the general with a copy of the verses and of Mrs. Willard's famous plan. So impressed was the general with his visit that he sent Emma an invitation to visit him and his family in France. This she was able to do during a trip to Europe some years later.

"I have some good news for you," announced Mrs. Willard at morning assembly one day in 1825. "The Erie Canal is to be opened in October. Governor Clinton has invited the entire school to celebrate the event by taking a trip through the locks."

The Erie Canal ran across the entire state of New York, connecting Albany to Buffalo. It opened the Midwest to commerce and trade with the East. Because it is near Albany, Troy prospered from the increased trade, and its population soon doubled. An elegant steamboat, the *Chief Justice Marshall,* plied the Hudson River between New York and Troy three times a week. Seminary graduates went all over the country to teach, and more pupils came to the seminary.

By 1830 the school was so well established that Emma was free to take a long trip to Europe. She visited French schools, and she also established a school in Athens, Greece, for the training of teachers. To help support this school, she later wrote a book about her travels, entitled *Journal from France and Great Britain.*

On the ship coming home from Europe, a terrible storm struck. Emma looked with concern at the rolling waves, the heaving decks, the lightning-streaked skies, and the unhappy passengers. Then, trying to keep calm, she retired to her cabin. In a short while, she composed the poem "Ocean Hymn." The next day it was set to music by a fellow passenger, and sung every evening thereafter by the entire company:

> Rocked in the cradle of the deep,
> I lay me down in peace to sleep;
> Secure I rest upon the wave
> For Thou, O Lord, hast power to save;
> I know Thou wilt not slight my call
> For Thou dost mark the sparrow's fall;
> And calm and peaceful is my sleep,
> Rocked in the cradle of the deep.

In this poem Emma was expressing her deep religious faith. This faith continued to support her during the next thirty years, as she worked to improve women's education. She wrote textbook after textbook. And she traveled widely, giving countless lectures, always urging the public to support female education and teacher training.

In 1838 she retired as headmistress at the Troy school and her son John took over its management. Although she continued her travels, she began to concentrate on improving the common schools in Connecticut. Soon she was chosen to be superintendent of the Kensington, Connecticut, schools, a position she held for four years. She attended the World's Educational Convention in London in 1845, representing the women of America.

In the 1820s and 1830s other women had begun to rally to Emma Willard's cause. Catharine Beecher set high standards in her Hartford Female Seminary, which had opened in 1823. Mary Lyon insisted on true college education for women and started Mount

Holyoke in 1837. As Mrs. Willard's graduates found positions throughout the country, they took their belief in quality education for women with them. Oberlin College gave degrees to women as well as men in 1837. Soon New York City and Boston began to provide public high schools for girls as well as boys.

Women were also clamoring for legal rights at the time, and they were becoming active in the abolitionist movement, which worked to do away with slavery. Emma, however, singlemindedly stuck to the field of education. And in this field she led the way. An article written in 1893 declared of her: "She laid the foundation upon which every woman's college or coeducational college may be said to rest."

At age seventy-four Emma Willard decided to retire, but she still found the energy three years later to draw up a universal peace plan which suggested a world judicial tribunal for solution of international disputes. Until her death in 1870, when she was eighty-three, she took part in the Troy school ceremonies.

In 1910, the school was renamed the Emma Willard School, and today it is a girls' preparatory school of high academic standing. It continues to follow the course she indicated in a speech in 1833: "That I have succeeded is owing much to the fact that I have looked forward to what *should be* in education rather than back, to imitate defective systems."

Emma Hart Willard had faith in women and faith in the future. This faith, expressed in a lifetime of work for quality education, is her legacy to mankind.

*Mary Lyon was the founder of Mount Holyoke College, the first permanent institution of higher learning for women.*

# A Noble School

## MARY LYON

*Founder of Mount Holyoke College.*

The family had gathered around the kitchen fire after supper. Mrs. Lyon was pushing the baby's cradle with one foot; her hands were busy with mending. Mr. Lyon was repairing a harness, and only the smallest of the seven children were idle as all listened to the tales Grandpa was telling.

"Well," Grandpa was saying, "when I was about eight or nine years old, I had a friend, an Indian boy, from the Algonquian tribe. His father had brought him along on a visit to Huntstown, where he was trading some skins for homespun and salt. The boy was hanging around the stockade, and he and I struck up an acquaintance. Nice fellow he was, too, named Red Deer. He taught me a lot about Indian ways."

"Tell us," chorused the children.

"The Algonquians were an artistic tribe," continued Grandpa. "They used birchbark to make their containers, bending it while it was wet and sewing it, then decorating it with pictures of animals, or even snowflakes. The women knew how to decorate their boxes and bags with porcupine quills, dyed a lot of pretty colors. Yessir, they made beautiful things."

He thought a minute or two.

"Well, Red Deer told me how the ground squirrel got his black stripes. Would you like to hear that story?"

"Of course, of course."

"Long ago, all the animals held a council. They were trying to decide how to divide the day between light and darkness. The bear was the biggest animal present, and he decided that it suited him to have the whole time dark — and he pronounced the decree.

"Much to his surprise, a little squirrel dared to speak up. 'It should be divided in half,' said the brave creature. 'Not all of us like the dark the way the bear does.'

"Several heads began to nod in agreement but quickly became still as the bear rose on his hind feet, reaching out an angry claw for the quivering squirrel. The bear's sharp claws scratched right down the squirrel's back and made those long black scars. But the squirrel managed to slide away to safety, and the other animals were so inspired by his bravery that they voted the bear down!

"Now, that's enough for tonight. Time for bed," said Grandpa as he finished his tale.

Little Mary Lyon, three years old, thought about the story as she climbed the stairs to her attic bed.

"I will be brave like the ground squirrel," she promised herself.

The Lyon family lived on a farm in western Massachusetts. Jemima and Aaron Lyon, Mary's parents, were of English stock, their ancestors having arrived with the earliest immigrants to New England. From

Ashfield, Massachusetts, the young couple had moved to Franklin County, settling in the village of Buckland in the foothills of the Hoosac Mountains. The children, six girls and a boy, came along quickly. Mary was born in 1797, and she was caring for her younger sisters before she was four years old.

On Sundays, the family went twice to church, as was the custom for the entire community. On the pulpit was an hourglass to be sure the parson preached at least an hour; sometimes he went on for an hour and a half. Discussion of the parson's sermon was an important part of Sunday dinner. Mr. Lyon liked to question his children to be sure that they were paying attention during the sermon.

Mary was bright and interested. She soon could quote much of the sermon from memory, and her sisters often relied on her to help them out.

"Quick, Mary, what did he say today?" one might whisper as they drove slowly home in the wagon.

"He was quoting from a sermon by the Reverend Samuel Willard," answered Mary. "It went like this: 'If one generation begins to decline, the next grows worse, and so on. . . . Alas! how doth vanity, and a fondness after new things abound among them? How do young persons grow weary of the strict profession of their fathers. . . .'" And Mary would continue right to the end of the sermon.

In 1802, when Mary was only five, her father died suddenly. His widow hid her grief and worked harder than ever to care for her young family. With the help of her son Aaron, then just thirteen, and a hired man, she continued to work their small farm.

For a few years Mary was privileged to learn her ABCs at the village school. With the help of her fine memory, she was soon walking up to the teacher's desk to recite. The teacher would point to the letters in her hornbook and Mary easily read: "$A\ b$ — ab; $E\ b$ —eb; $I\ b$ — ib; $O\ b$ — ob; $U\ b$ —ub."

From the very beginning, Mary loved school and was eager to learn everything she could. But the education provided by village schools in those days was limited and irregular. None of the schools near Buckland were permanent. They closed down if the teacher left, or they moved to a new town with him. When she could not go to school, Mary stayed at home and helped her mother. By the time she was thirteen, she was as competent in the farm woman's crafts as anyone twice her age.

One of the important tasks Mary had to learn was spinning. She and her sisters would prepare the wool for spinning after a neighboring farmer had helped shear their sheep. First, they put the wool into bags and washed it in a tub of water for a few minutes. Then it was spread out to dry. The older girls carded the wool on paddles with bent wires set into them, drawing the fibers back and forth until the wool became soft and fluffy, ready to be made into yarn. Mary would seat herself at the spinning wheel and pull out two or three inches of fiber at a time, allowing the wheel to twist the fibers into yarn. As her nimble fingers guided the yarn and her feet pumped the treadle, her mind was free to dream. Mary's dreams were always about going to another school. She was determined to get more schooling, somehow.

When Mary was thirteen, her mother remarried and moved to Ashfield. Mary decided to stay on at the farm and keep house for her brother Aaron. For this he paid her a dollar a week, and everything she earned went into a special fund—her Education Fund.

Over the next few years, she was able to add to her Education Fund by doing spinning and weaving for other families. Although she was young, she became an assistant teacher in the village school, and was paid seventy-five cents a week. Then, in 1817, when Mary was nineteen, she heard of the opportunity she had been waiting for. A new academy for girls was opening in Ashfield, taught by a college graduate — so the training promised to be more advanced than any she had had up to that time. She gathered up her savings and entered the new Sanderson Academy. At last she was going back to school!

Walking briskly from church on her first Sunday in Ashfield, Mary fell in step with another young woman, who said, "I'm Amanda White. Are you going to Sanderson Academy, too?"

"Oh yes!" exclaimed Mary, introducing herself. "It's the happiest day of my life!"

Her bright blue eyes sparkled and her curly auburn hair bobbed up and down beneath her cap. She continued, "Tell me, have you ever had a course in mathematics? You have? Would you be able to lend me your book? It is a subject I know very little about."

"Of course," replied Amanda, charmed by Mary's open, friendly manner and curious about this young woman who dressed in strange, old-fashioned clothes and wanted to study mathematics on her own.

"I knew you must be a good person," she explained to Mary many months later, "because I could tell you cared nothing for your appearance!"

When Mary had walked to her chapel seat on opening day at Sanderson, the other students had laughed at her a little: her homespun dress looked much like a sack; the ties to her cap were undone; her country shoes were heavy and clumsy. But after a few days they recognized her brilliant mind and open manner, and they accepted her as a friend. She was always willing to lend a hand to any student who needed help with lessons, or who just needed a sympathetic listener.

And Amanda — what a friend she proved to be! Amanda's parents grew to love Mary as their own daughter. Mr. White was a trustee of the academy, and when Mary's limited funds ran out, he persuaded the trustees to give her free tuition, and the Whites welcomed her into their own home to live.

After graduating from Sanderson Academy, Mary supported herself by teaching, and between school terms continued her education at Byfield Female Seminary. This school was led by the Reverend Joseph Emerson, a cousin of the famous Ralph Waldo Emerson. He was an important influence on Mary, because he believed in education for women, and because he encouraged students to develop their intellectual abilities.

After Byfield, Mary returned to Sanderson Academy as its first woman teacher. Because there were so few qualified women teachers then, Mary was in great demand, and when she could she taught in various village schools nearby. In 1824, after several terms as a teacher at Sanderson, Mary began teaching summers at Adams Academy in New Hampshire. The academy was run by Zilpah Grant, a friend of Mary's from Byfield days. In the winter, she ran her own female seminary in Buckland. This school was particularly successful and increased Mary's reputation as a teacher.

In 1828 she accepted an invitation to teach at Ipswich Female Seminary in Ipswich, Massachusetts. This school, which had been started by Zilpah Grant, provided advanced training for women. Zilpah and Mary made a perfect team. Between them, the seminary prospered, and was soon attracting students from many states. So well-trained were the graduates that they became sought after as teachers in schools across the country.

One day, Mary talked to Zilpah about an idea that had been steadily growing in her mind.

"I want to start my own college for girls," she explained. "What we are doing here at Ipswich is fine, but our school is not permanent. I want my school to have a firm foundation as do the men's colleges. It will not be dependent on the fortunes or lives of a few persons or private businesses. These withdraw their support as soon as the school stops paying dividends. Instead, my school must be publicly funded. It must provide such a good example in higher education for women that people will want to support other such institutions all over the country."

It was an ambitious course that Mary had set for herself. She and Zilpah both knew what a struggle it had been to get funds for the Ipswich school. The public was simply not concerned about higher education for girls. But Mary believed strongly that the country needed educated women. She also believed that all women should have an opportunity for advanced schooling, not just the wealthy ones. The school she was planning would be for the middle class, for people without a lot of money. Although the idea of a permanent college for women was new and revolutionary, Mary was certain that she could succeed.

"Will you help me, Zilpah? Will you help me plan?"

"Yes, of course I'll help you, Mary. Though I

don't know how Ipswich will get along without you."

"I will spend the summer visiting other schools and making plans," said Mary. "But I won't leave Ipswich until you find someone else to replace me."

Mary spent the summer of 1833 traveling around to various schools to learn what they were doing. She was well known as an educator by that time, and a committee of citizens from the city of Detroit invited her to found her school there. But Miss Lyon refused, reasoning, "Massachusetts has been the fount of education since the Pilgrims arrived in 1620. If my little enterprise should succeed there, it will be copied everywhere. And surely I shall find a sympathetic reception among the cultured citizens of my native state."

During her last year at Ipswich, she worked out her plan, and circulated it among the citizens of Ipswich.

"I plan to establish a residential seminary to be founded and sustained by the Christian public," she wrote, "board and tuition at cost or as low as it may be, domestic work to be performed by its family, surplus income going into the treasury, teachers contributing cheerfully their services at very moderate salaries."

Her plan also emphasized that her seminary would own its own property and exist under the direction of an unpaid board of trustees, who would elect their own successors. Thus the institution would not depend on the life or fortune of one individual.

Mary knew, however, that she would not be able to accomplish her goal without help. She did not dare to go around making speeches in front of mixed audiences, because people would criticize her conduct so much that she would have no chance of succeeding. So she asked several influential men to help her. In September, 1834, Mary met with a group of these men at Ipswich Seminary, and outlined her plan for a new college for women.

Her listeners had in recent years become aware that many of the farmers and tradespeople of the eastern states would soon follow the pioneers out west if better opportunities were not provided for them at home. Steam and machinery were bringing change; factory workers would need some education, and there must be enough teachers to provide it. Women teachers would be needed more and more. Thus education had to be for women, too.

Mary Lyon touched on all these points. She also emphasized the American goal of opportunity for all. She was a persuasive speaker. At this meeting, the men appointed a committee of seven to act as a temporary board of trustees for the proposed new college. The board was given the power to add to its own membership, fill any vacancies, and represent the enterprise before the public. It was decided that after a charter had been drawn up for the school, ten permanent trustees would be named.

One of the gentlemen declared, "My friends, we must have at least a thousand dollars in public funds, first, to assist in raising the main amount, and second, so that people will be sure their gifts would not be used in any degree to pay for agents or advertising."

Miss Lyon agreed. She felt so strongly that her cause was a good one, and that people everywhere would support it, that she volunteered to raise the first thousand dollars herself.

The men were doubtful that she could succeed, but she insisted. "Gentlemen, you have done your part for now. It is my turn; let me proceed."

And with that the meeting was adjourned.

Students and teachers at Ipswich quickly raised about two hundred and fifty dollars.

"That was too easy," said Miss Lyon to herself. The next day, she took to the streets. Knocking on the first door, she startled the man who opened it with her rapid-fire introduction:

"I am Mary Lyon, of Ipswich Seminary. I have a matter of the utmost importance to speak about with the mistress of the house. Would it be convenient to beg a few moments of her time?"

"Of course, of course, Miss Lyon. Please come in."

As soon as she was led into the parlor, Miss Lyon began to speak. She sat on the edge of the horsehair sofa, addressing her remarks to the woman while the husband lighted the fire.

"Madam," she said earnestly, "I need your help; I need it most desperately. Some gentlemen have agreed to help me establish a seminary for young women that will afford them a liberal education such as that now available to their brothers. And at a price which the daughters of our community can well afford.

"I know that women do not have substantial means to invest in such a project. They have no property, no bank accounts, no share in business enterprises. But, Madam, when you have wanted a new carpet, or a picture for your parlor, have you not somehow managed to obtain it? We all have our little ways to save money, have we not? So now I ask you — I offer you the opportunity — to invest in the future of our daughters, yours and mine, kin whether by blood or only by sex. What do you say?"

Miss Lyon's bright eyes, enthusiastic voice, and persuasive manner soon charmed the good housewives of Ipswich. Out of sugar bowls and from under mattresses came nickels, dimes, and half-dollars. House by house, block by block, walked Miss Lyon, day after day. She skipped no home, reasoning that all women would benefit from her plan; therefore, all should have a chance to participate.

Thus it was that one afternoon she rapped gently on the door of an unpainted little cottage on the outskirts of town. The woman who answered was thin and her face worn, though she was fairly young. In one arm she held a baby; the other she raised to push back a falling strand of hair.

"You are busy, I know," said Miss Lyon after introducing herself. "But I wonder if I might hold the baby and talk to you while you go about your other duties."

The woman smiled hesitantly.

"Why, I guess you can come in," she said.

Miss Lyon began, "I want to talk to you about education — women's education."

The woman's eyes lighted up for an instant.

"I always thought I could've done right well in school," she said. "I learned my letters quickly and could recite the catechism as well as anybody in school. But I couldn't stay; there was too much to do on the farm. And then I got married — my husband works at the sawmill. He tries hard, but with seven children. . . ."

"Well, it is just possible that your girls may be able to go to a school such as the one I am proposing. Let me tell you about it."

She explained her dream, stressing the low cost of the school, the possibility of scholarships, the benefits to children who might later be taught by the well-trained graduates.

"Would you like to help such an enterprise?" she concluded.

"Miss Lyon," the woman answered, "I do want to help. I wish I could give you lots of money. But the only money I have," she said, reaching into a nearby drawer and pulling forth a long black stocking, "is these three pennies given me by a woman I stayed the night with when she was sick. I was aiming to buy myself something pretty with it, but now I want to give it to you for your school."

And she handed over the pennies. Miss Lyon's eyes were bright with unshed tears.

"Oh, it is just like the widow's mite in the Bible!" she exclaimed. "And God will bless you for your generosity. It will mean more to our school than a gift of hundreds of dollars. Thank you, thank you! And when our school opens, you must pay me a visit; I will take you on a personal tour."

As she walked on down the street, Miss Lyon's feet did a little skip on the muddy road.

"It is a happy omen," she said to herself. "Now I know we will get our thousand dollars."

Within two months, she had the money in hand. The trustees met again to launch a campaign throughout the state to raise twenty-five thousand dollars for the actual building.

Miss Lyon doubled her efforts. She spoke to small groups of men, inviting their advice and cooperation. By jolting stagecoach she rode from town to town, asking for subscriptions and donations. The college town of Amherst became her headquarters; she found lodgings in the home of a sympathetic professor. Here she worked out in detail her principles of female education. They included three main points: (1) to secure for young women, as for young men, training to fit them for serving society; (2) to equalize the opportunity for this training; (3) to do these things now. Her emphasis on providing education for women at public expense was a unique one for her day.

Education, she said, was to be guided by "the wants of the great mass of the community rather than of a few families, and training would aim at the complete woman — physically, mentally, and spiritually developed; a Christian school, but non-denominational."

Tireless, Mary Lyon worked on her curriculum, served as consultant for the new Wheaton Seminary for girls, and conferred with her trustees on the subject of a proper site for the school. Finally, they chose a location near the Connecticut River in western Massachusetts. The mountain rising nearby gave its name to the seminary, and on February 11, 1836, the governor signed Mount Holyoke's charter. In just a few weeks the trustees began looking at architects' fees and plans.

At that very time, however, financial clouds were forming over the United States, troubles that would result in the Panic of 1837. The twenty-five-thousand-dollar goal could not be met by the appointed time. Some of the trustees seemed ready to abandon the project. Miss Lyon refused to give up, but she did agree to delay the date for starting construction.

Finally, in October, 1836, the building's cornerstone was laid. Miss Lyon made frequent trips to oversee construction. On one such visit, the walls of the newly laid foundation collapsed. Crash! The bricks came tumbling down. The foreman came rushing from his breakfast to survey the damage.

"Oh, how I hate to tell Miss Lyon!" he said aloud.

But she was hurrying toward him, smiling happily.

"How fortunate that all the men were at breakfast!" she exclaimed. "They could have been gravely injured!"

What workmen would not respond to such a woman? They all tried their best to please her, and the work progressed steadily.

There was hardly enough money to keep the construction going, much less to buy furnishings. But Miss Lyon knew exactly what to do. Dozens of letters went out, to friends and to friends of friends. Each little town that showed interest was given the furnishing of a single room as its own project; extra contributions went into a general furniture fund. One man furnished a room in memory of his daughter. Crockery was promised by another. Little gifts, big gifts.

However, many of the pledges continued to be postponed, because of the economic situation. The twenty-five thousand dollars had not been raised.

"Let's wait another year or two," said some of the trustees.

"Never!" said Miss Lyon, and worked even harder. Like a master juggler she interviewed prospective students and teachers, collected furniture money, and kept the construction going, all at the same time.

November 8 was announced as opening date, and seventy-eight students had been accepted into the first class. They were asked to bring what furnishings they could, and on the appointed day the carriages began to arrive. Fathers brought their daughters, all seventeen or older, and carried their trunks. Walking into the red brick Georgian building of four stories, they saw dignified men tacking matting to the floors; a renowned trustee, assisted by students, was laying carpet; and the dainty wife of another was washing dishes. Miss Lyon herself fixed breakfast the next morning. Soon each girl was assigned to a task, for this boarding school was to provide little outside help: the girls did most of the work. The cooperation that was demanded of them made them feel close to each other and loyal to their school. Miss Lyon so thoroughly organized the duties and activities of the school that soon she was able to trust the students to carry through on their own.

"It was a daily object lesson in system and order, a beautiful example of successful cooperative housekeeping," she later wrote. "Teamwork and leadership are its inevitable results."

Before being accepted, each student had been thoroughly examined in English grammar, modern geography, United States history, and arithmetic. The seminary provided a regular course of three years. There were quiet hours for contemplation at the beginning and end of each day. Walking and calisthenics were also included in the program.

Mount Holyoke Female Seminary was an immediate success. Three hundred applicants had to be turned down the second year. An addition to the building was begun right away. Miss Lyon was content.

One day in 1838 there was a knock on her door. In came a group of students bearing a large birthday cake with lighted candles. They presented her with a large, handsomely wrapped package. Inside lay two stylish new caps: Miss Lyon was still wearing the turbans that had been in vogue fifteen years before. Doubtless she had never noticed the style change. For the school's first commencement, she was gently persuaded to purchase a new silk gown. It lasted through many succeeding commencements.

However, not everyone had accepted the idea of

college education for women; some skeptics still existed. After attending a graduation exercise, the *Boston Traveler* reporter wrote:

> The teachers and pupils seemed good-humored and happy. . . . Some of the lighter accomplishments, as drawing, music and embroidery, were either not exhibited, or evidently not made very prominent in the course of instruction. . . . The public conferring of degrees, however, is an evil, slight in itself, but leading to others, and endangering that beautiful seclusion in which female loveliness should live and move, and have both its being and its rewards. Twelve young ladies, without parents, rising in a crowded church to receive a broad diploma with its collegiate seal, presented to my view the least attractive spectacle of a most interesting day. . . . But it is a noble school, and will certainly flourish.

And flourish it did. Mary Lyon at last was able to delegate some responsibility and to pay attention to her own failing health. With a niece in 1841 she made a sentimental journey through the countryside of her youth. Out of this trip came her only book, a moving account of her early farm life, called *A Missionary Offering*.

The book illustrates how important her religious beliefs were to Mary Lyon. "Say little, pray much," she advised her students. "Let love through all our actions run, in every deed, look, work, or thought." She herself spent many moments in prayer, and her own Christian life was her best sermon. She gave at least a third of her small salary to missionary work and inspired many of her students to also give generous contributions.

"Sit with energy," she had often advised her students. But her own energy began to lessen. One spring she became seriously ill, following a severe cold. Although she made an apparent recovery, a few weeks later, on March 5, 1849, she suddenly died. The active body, the alert mind, were stilled.

But her school, in spite of many more years of financial struggle, managed to endure. Her courageous ideas spread into the entire educational field, helping to destroy skepticism about the intellectual abilities of women. Almost singlehandedly, in the face of hostility and ridicule, this determined woman had pursued her idea until it became a practical expression. The name of Mount Holyoke was changed many years later from seminary to college. It remains today one of the great colleges for women.

*A zoology lab in the 1890s. Mount Holyoke continued to offer quality education even after Mary Lyon's death.*

*Martha Berry, founder of Berry College, worked to bring education to the poor children of the Appalachian Mountains.*

# Nobody Dared Say No

## MARTHA BERRY

*Educator in the Appalachian Mountains.*

The setting sun magnified the shadows of the branches of the stately oaks and pines, and the dignified white columns of the house bore unemotional witness to the drama being played out in the parlor. Inside this formal room, heavily curtained against the summer heat, a pretty young woman stood face to face with a Virginia gentleman. Her blue eyes were flashing as she regarded her suitor. His voice, though carefully controlled, reflected his frustration and disappointment. Their words, however, could not be heard beyond the thick doors, and the participants in this drama thereafter kept its secrets to themselves.

Suddenly, the sisters in the living room, the parents in their upstairs bedroom, and the servants in the kitchen became aware of heavy footsteps striding hastily out the entrance hall and the loud slam of the front door. Then they heard Martha Berry running to the privacy of her room.

"What has happened?" wondered her sisters as they came out into the hall in time to see the young man fling himself upon his horse and gallop away into the night. Mrs. Berry hurried down the stairs and joined her daughters on the side veranda. From an upstairs window of Martha's room came the sound of uncontrollable sobbing.

Mrs. Berry gave a long sigh. "I'm afraid that romance is finished," she said quietly. Then, as Frances started toward Martha's room, she stretched forth a restraining hand.

"Leave her alone for now," she said. "She will want to get control of herself before she talks to anybody."

And so Martha was left to cry herself to sleep. Next morning, red-eyed and solemn, she appeared at the breakfast table. One of the girls spoke up.

"Oh, Martha, did you send him away for good?"

"It is all over," said Martha in a resolute voice. "We will not speak of it again."

She kept her word, giving no reason for breaking her five-year engagement to the young man from Virginia. However, she probably realized that she could never be a conventional Southern matron. That life would not mix with her dream — establishing a school for Appalachian mountain boys.

It was a highly unusual choice, especially for her day, but it resulted in an incredible achievement. This Southern lady displayed a singleminded purpose that carried her to national fame and won her the enduring gratitude of her mountain neighbors.

To be sure, on the night when she parted company with her young man, her school was little more than a dream. But she was already involved in trying to provide some education for children of the Appalachian mountaineers. She surely recognized the fact that marriage would have interfered with her plans, so she chose to remain single.

The atmosphere in which Martha Berry grew up seemed unlikely to produce a woman with such plans. She was born on October 7, 1866, in Rome, Georgia, a small town trying to recover from the devastating effects of the Civil War. The entire county numbered only about eighteen thousand persons, but to serve this population of whites and newly freed blacks, the little town boasted fine brick stores up and down Broad Street. The Rome Railroad Company and the Selma, Rome and Dalton Railway maintained a busy schedule of both freight and passenger trains. Riverboat traffic was also active.

Two newspapers, the *Courier* and the *Commercial,* provided local and national news, and they advertised the latest fashions for the benefit of the women. These fashions could easily be copied by clever seamstresses into lovely gowns, and Patrick and Ormberg's department store handled a large supply of yard goods, laces, and ribbons. The Misses Attaway and Wilkinson created beautiful hats to order. For recreation, there were socials organized by the four leading churches; a dancing academy; billiard parlors and lodge and grange meetings for the men; and riverboat excursions on the lovely Coosa River.

Rome's location was excellent for future growth. Nestled at the foothills of the Appalachian Mountains, it also lay at the fork of the Etowah and Oostanaula rivers, which form the wide and sparkling Coosa. Both Atlanta and Chattanooga were only hours away by train.

When Captain Thomas Berry returned to Rome with his wife and one small daughter at the close of the

Civil War, he found his plantation house, Oak Hill, still intact although his financial resources had been wiped out. His wife sold her jewelry to finance a trip to New York, where Berry's prewar reputation for integrity and hard work produced a loan of fifty thousand dollars from some wealthy Easterners. Within a few years, the captain was again on his feet. As each of the eight children came along, with stairstep regularity, he was able to provide a comfortable living for them. Also, Captain Berry cared for the three children of a deceased sister as well.

As offspring of a prominent Georgia family, the Berry children enjoyed many social benefits. The oldest daughter, Jennie, loved the local fairs and the programs given by visiting actors and musicians. Martha, too, took part in the social events that became more frequent as the girls reached their teens.

Since the state of Georgia provided little public education at this time, the girls depended on the effectiveness of the private tutors engaged by the captain. One of these, Ida McCullough, was especially beloved by Martha. She introduced the teenage girls to the wonders of nature, teaching Martha to spot the exquisite wild flowers peeping forth from their winter blanket of leaves; to recognize the hanging nest of the flying squirrel, whose webbed feet enabled it to soar like a bird from tree to tree; to examine the box turtle as it slowly made its way across a rustic path, securely housed in its fortress shell.

Martha was especially close to her father. And he was the one who introduced her to the mountain people. He made a point of calling on former soldiers whom he had known, offering them a helping hand in the form of a loan, a used plow, or a simple word of encouragement. Martha often accompanied him on rides through the mountains.

On such a trip one day she brought up a new idea.

"Father, I wish you would do something special for us children," she begged. "I believe I would like school even better if we could have classes in a little log cabin, just like that one we just passed. I don't like being cooped up in the house."

"For my children's education, I'll do everything humanly possible," agreed the captain.

True to his word, within a few weeks a neat little cabin arose not far from the big house. Here the children had their lessons, and here Martha tried to control her impatience to be up and away on her pony, roaming the foothills and mountain passes.

At age sixteen Martha was sent away to Madame LeFebre's finishing school in Baltimore. There were local preparatory schools, such as Hearn Academy and Mr. Holleyman's School for Girls, but well-to-do Rome families preferred to send their daughters to fashionable schools in Washington or Baltimore.

Martha was very unhappy at Madame's school. Her bleached petticoats and long-sleeved gowns were less stylish than those of her schoolmates; she sensed that she did not quite fit in.

"I'm coming home," she wrote her father.

"If you do, you will promptly be returned," he wired back. "A project undertaken must be carried to its conclusion."

At his suggestion, however, the headmistress took Martha shopping for new clothes, and she was a little less unhappy. But that year marked the end of her schooling.

She returned to Oak Hill when her father became

ill. Soon he was confined to a wheelchair, and Martha spent many hours at his side. But she still had time for her pony and for excursions into the surrounding countryside. She also entered into the social activities of the hospitable community. Beaux and parties became a regular part of her life.

When the young Virginian won her heart, the entire community rejoiced. Her family also was pleased with the match and was sorry when it did not last.

But Captain Berry did not recover his health. One day he called Martha to his side. "Martha, I am leaving you that land across the road — nearly a hundred acres," he said. "Never give it up; as long as you own land, you will never starve."

Soon after, Martha's father died. He had left her the land, but also another gift; through him she had learned to appreciate and understand the mountain people. He had shown her how to help them in ways that would not arouse their proud resistance to charity.

Her father had a favorite verse from Psalms that she adopted as her own: "The lines have fallen unto me in pleasant places. Yea, I have a goodly heritage."

But a nagging worry persisted in the back of her mind. "Yes, I have a 'goodly heritage' — but what should I do with it? I am not sure I want a life like my mother's: tending a household of servants and children, planning meals, being bored at gossipy teas and church socials."

The answer came suddenly, but its meaning was not apparent at the time.

"I had a dream," she reminisced in later life. "I had a dream, just like those prophets in the Bible. But my dream was real. It was three little tattered mountain boys. They appeared suddenly, just as angels often did.

But they certainly didn't look much like angels!

"I was down in my little cabin one Sunday afternoon, reading. I happened to look up to see three dirty little faces peering in my window. I immediately went to the door and invited the little urchins in. At first they were shy, but the proffer of an apple lured them in. I motioned for them to sit down and, for want of anything better to say, I asked them if they had been to Sunday school that morning.

" 'We-uns ain't got no Sunday school,' explained one. 'We have church sometime when the preacher kin git around t'us.'

" 'Then perhaps you would like for me to tell you a Bible story,' I suggested.

" 'Yessum, we'd shore like that,' responded the older child."

Martha had an expressive face, an enthusiastic voice, and dramatic instincts. She launched into the story of Adam and Eve and was rewarded by the rapt attention of her listeners. And so for an hour Martha spun the Bible tales she had learned in her own Episcopal Sunday School.

It was growing dusk when she finally urged the boys to go home.

"But come back next Sunday and I'll tell you some more stories," she promised.

"Can we bring our sisters?" asked the oldest boy.

"Of course," answered Martha. "Bring anybody you want to."

On the following Sunday the trio reappeared, leading two little sisters by the hand. Martha was prepared with her stories, but she also had other plans. She had brought with her a magnifying glass left over from her school days with Miss McCullough.

"Put your hand under this glass," she ordered each child in turn. "Look at all that dirt in your skin; imagine the millions of germs hiding under those dirty fingernails. What if they should get into your mouth? That is how people get sick.

"Now, scrub your hands and faces with this soap and water. We have plenty of towels, too. Then look through the microscope again. It won't look like the same skin!"

Like the Pied Piper, Miss Berry soon was attracting children from miles away. Hymn singing and Bible stories were the order of the day. Soon the cabin became too small and Martha began looking for a larger place. She was beginning to refer to them as "my children," and her family became alarmed. Her mother tried to tell her that she was spending too much time with them and that it would be no use in the long run. But Martha remembered how the children's faces lighted up when they listened to her Bible stories, and she kept on.

The family had trouble keeping quiet, however, when they looked out the kitchen window one Sunday. Descending on the spotless lawn of Oak Hill was a motley assortment of buggies, wagons, and mules. People of all ages appeared, plus a dozen or more hound dogs that sniffed around the beautiful box bushes and chased each other through the shrubbery.

Martha Berry rushed out to meet them, wondering what was happening.

One of the men slid off his mule, bowed slightly to her, and spoke hesitantly.

"I be Floy Austin's paw. We-uns come to thank you for teachin' our chillun and cleanin' 'em up, too. We appreciate it mightily, and we jes' wanted to tell you how you-uns has helped us." He waved his hand to include the whole group.

Martha Berry rose instantly to the occasion.

"That's mighty kind of you, Mr. Austin. Won't you stay awhile till our Sunday school class is over?"

She made a hurried trip to the kitchen to ask the servants to prepare some tea and cookies, then had the boys pull the old melodeon out on the lawn. Soon the mountain voices were singing enthusiastically. "Onward, Christian Soldiers," "Love Lifted Me," "America, the Beautiful," "John Brown's Body" — for an hour or more the joyful sounds rang out. Martha recited two Bible stories, then, after a final song, invited her guests to enjoy the simple refreshments.

Her sleep that night was restless. The next morning, she mounted her pony and began a search. When she spotted a neglected old church building some eight miles away, on the Possum Trot Road, she found an answer — and the answer to her life's purpose as well.

Martha quickly spread the news that next Sunday's meeting would be at the Possum Trot church, and that everyone should come. It was raining when the mountaineers assembled the next Sunday, and it became clear that the building needed some work. After the Sunday school was over, Miss Berry addressed her audience.

"We are going to fix up this building," she announced. "I am inviting all of you to a 'workin' next Wednesday. I'll bring lemonade and cookies — and nails. We are not going to have another meeting under a leaking roof."

Somewhat to her surprise, the men appeared on Wednesday, worked hard all day, and finished the job.

"Fust time I ever seed a woman bossin' a house

roofin'," remarked one of them in amazement as he accepted a welcome glass of cold lemonade. It was not the last time this lady was to boss men.

In the hills, Martha Berry quickly became famous as the "Sunday lady"; her pony even was known as the "Sunday horse." She soon was called on to organize another Sunday school in the Mount Alto community, then another at Foster's Bend, twenty miles down the Coosa River.

That year, she invited all the students to a Christmas party at her log cabin. When the day came, the crowd began drifting in by ten o'clock, far more numerous than expected. Hastily Martha and her sisters began wrapping extra presents. They raided every drawer in the house. Hair ribbons, neckties, lace collars, handkerchiefs, canned goods — anything, everything. It was the first real Christmas many of the children had ever observed, and their excited response was overwhelming.

When the party was over and the last straggler gone, Martha sat exhausted in her little cabin. She could not get the children out of her mind. What chance did they have in the world of the brand new century? And what could she do about the problem? Sunday school once a week was not enough. School, real school, was what these children needed. The state of Georgia with its limited funds offered only about a half-dozen public schools and then for five months a year. Even these few schools were usually too far away for the hill children to reach.

A lone woman like herself could not possibly solve a problem like this. She had little formal education and few resources. Resolutely, Martha dismissed the problem from her mind.

But the plight of the people would not leave her thought.

"I would ride my pony for miles through a zigzag path in the resinous woods, leading up to some isolated little cabin. The whole family would come out to welcome us. And the words grew quite familiar: 'Yonder comes the Sunday lady! Hitch yo' nag and 'light — 'light and come in. We-uns be pow-ful glad to see you.' " Thus Miss Berry later described her trips.

Generous in their poverty, appreciative of her efforts with their children, the simple highlanders had aroused her concern. But she also received great satisfaction in being able to reach them. For they have always been a proud lot, these Appalachians. Mostly from Scotland and Ireland, their ancestors had left the British Isles in the 1600s and 1700s, arriving in Pennsylvania and Virginia and streaming down into the Carolinas, Georgia, and Tennessee. Their part in winning the Revolutionary War had been extensive. Afterwards, they had retired to their small mountain farms to enjoy the liberties for which they had fought. But they knew nothing of scientific agriculture; the crops grew smaller and smaller as the soil grew poorer; schools were scarce or nonexistent; and lack of roads between the mountainous farms hindered communication.

Slowly, they sank into poverty. Their contacts with the prospering world of the United States grew fewer, and their native intelligence sometimes was reduced by intermarriage and by disease and malnutrition. To earn enough for necessities, some of the mountain people took up "moonshining," that is, making whiskey, which they sold tax free. Their fellow Southerners, trying to regain their prewar prosperity, ignored the mountain people, and the mountaineers became increasingly proud and suspicious of strangers.

But they had accepted the Sunday lady. And she felt a real obligation toward them. Soon Martha reached a decision. She would begin with a school for the mountain boys. It would not be just a Sunday school, but a real day school, where the boys could learn reading and writing and perhaps cleanliness and nutrition. In a short time she had organized not one but five day schools in the mountain communities. Her sister Frances and a few friends helped with the teaching, learning the best methods by trial and error. Eventually Miss Berry persuaded the county superintendent of education to staff the schools; she herself paid the teacher for an extra month, in order to make the term six months long.

As the second year began, Martha became a little discouraged. When the children returned in the fall after the six months' vacation, they seemed to have forgotten nearly everything they had learned. Attendance, also, was uncertain; bad weather, a crisis in farming, or no excuse at all kept the children at home.

"I must get them out of that environment," she realized. "I shall start a boarding school, where the boys can work to pay their way. I cannot allow this generation of children to be lost."

With that decision she set the course of her life.

It took several weeks of hard thinking for her to come up with a plan. Finally, however, she was ready to pay a visit to the family lawyer.

"I am going to start a school for mountain boys," she announced, "and I want to deed to the school the land my father left me. Will you see to it at once?"

The lawyer gasped.

"Martha, do you realize what you are undertaking? How small the chance it has for success? The lack of financial security you will have when it fails?"

To his arguments and to those of her family a few hours later, Martha was unyielding.

"I must try. It is what I want more than anything else in the world. And I have enough money for one building."

And so Martha Berry started the Boys Industrial School. It opened on January 13, 1902, with a total of five students. For weeks before, Martha had ridden through the mountains, talking to the parents of boys she considered promising. She explained that the boys could pay for their board and tuition by working at the school, both during the term and during vacations. Within a week, two more students appeared, and by the end of the year eighteen were enrolled.

The program the boys followed was carefully planned to fit their needs. They learned to read, write, and do arithmetic, but that was not all. The boys also were taught the latest methods for growing crops and raising livestock. Lack of knowledge about modern agriculture had kept their parents in poverty; the boys at B.I.S., Martha decided, would be able to do better.

The school building, designed by an architect friend, was on a small rise opposite Oak Hill. It cost twenty-five hundred dollars. The furnishings were hand-me-downs from local attics. A friend contributed an old piano. Answering an ad in the paper, Miss Berry bought army cots at a bargain price, only to discover that they were too short for her lanky students. A packing case at the foot of each bed remedied that problem.

Incredibly, the school acquired a teacher. Miss Berry had advertised for one, and Elizabeth Brewster, a recent graduate of Stanford University, had accepted the position. In gratitude, the founder named the first building Brewster Hall.

During opening week, a major crisis occurred. Since there was no money to spend for services of any kind, Miss Berry informed the students that they would have to wash their own clothes. She brought a wash basin, a bucket of well water, and soap.

"Well, who wants to be first?" she inquired brightly.

There was a hushed silence.

Finally, one youngster spoke up.

"Washin' clothes — that's women's work!" he exclaimed scornfully.

Martha Berry looked at each one in turn. No one said a word.

"Very well. I shall have to do it myself. Hand me your shirts."

The boys glanced at each other in an abashed manner. Miss Berry continued to hold out her hand.

The oldest and biggest boy picked up the bar of soap.

"I guess I can wash my own," he said in a resigned tone of voice.

From then on, every project was a cooperative effort. The boys plowed the fields, dug drainage ditches, and planted windbreaks. They grew vegetables and grain crops. Soon they had added sides and a back to the school building, which included a small chapel. These projects helped the school, but they also taught the boys many valuable skills.

As part of their tuition payment, some students had brought a cow, a pig, mules, or even a yoke of oxen. Few had cash money. Miss Berry began to realize that she must secure additional financial help in order to keep her school going. She contacted everybody she knew in Rome and also a few friends in Atlanta. One of them, John Egan, agreed to head up a board of trustees. The school was showing promise of success, but expenses also increased. Miss Berry kept expanding her fund raising efforts. Thus began many years of tireless work for her dream — knocking on doors, writing letters, and giving speeches.

In the spring, she began to plan for the first commencement. The Honorable Hoke Smith, a former Secretary of the Interior now active in Georgia politics, accepted Miss Berry's cordial invitation to speak. A few days after she had written him, disaster struck. The schoolhouse — the beautiful, lovingly built schoolhouse — burned to the ground.

Miss Berry was the first to rally.

"We will hold the exercises in the yard," she announced. "Let us make it a beautiful occasion."

A steady downpour of rain on the appointed day made it necessary to borrow a tent from a local revival preacher. Miss Berry personally escorted the speaker from the train depot. As they drove along the rainswept driveway, Mr. Smith looked around him.

"But where is the school, Miss Berry?"

She explained what had happened.

"What a shame!" he sympathized. "And how many are in your graduating class, Miss Berry?"

"One. But he is a very unusual boy. He is sure to go far. He is the class valedictorian, and the honor graduate, too!"

Mr. Smith smiled thoughtfully and said no more. A huge crowd had assembled to listen to an oratorical contest. Mr. Smith received an ovation. So impressed was he by the entire event that he made a substantial contribution toward a dormitory and in time became a member of the board of trustees.

By the beginning of the second year, the school had room for sixty boys. A few more teachers had been added also. The work-study idea was proving itself. Word of the "Berry miracle" began to reach the outside world, and visitors became commonplace. The county superintendents of education in Georgia held a conference on campus to study Miss Berry's methods. Scientific ideas for improving agriculture, developed at the school, were carried into the surrounding areas.

Lack of money continued to be a critical problem. Remembering her father's successful effort to obtain financial help in the East, Martha Berry reluctantly put aside her distaste for public begging and went to New York.

One of her friends from the Baltimore finishing school introduced her to a minister, who invited her to speak to his congregation in Brooklyn. Unsure of the way and hindered by a blizzard, she arrived just as the service was ending. Nevertheless, she was allowed to make her plea.

She told her New York audience humorous, often moving, stories about her mountain boys. She talked about the families who sacrificed their livestock to pay for their sons' tuition. She described a Sunday dinner she had enjoyed at the home of a student whose mother said that "Ben scrubbed with so much vigor that the floors are still quite damp. . . . He'd rather scrub than eat!"

"They only want the chance that others have every day," she concluded.

Many of her listeners made donations. One gave

her the name of a New York industrialist, R. Fulton Cutting. Martha contacted him as soon as she could, and when she received a chance to convince him of the justice of her cause, she succeeded beyond her expectations.

"How much salary do you make?" he asked.

"Why, none. We can't afford to pay me anything."

She left with a check for five hundred dollars and the promise of continued support.

In 1907, when the Boys Industrial School was five years old, it was clear that it had proved itself. There were 150 students and six buildings. The campus had also grown, as Martha had begun her lifelong program of purchasing neighborhood land when it became available.

Martha Berry was a firm Christian; she had faith in her project and spent much time in prayer. But she did not let her faith stand alone; she assisted it with all her being. Her great persistence is illustrated by the following experience: One day she was invited to a gala reception in Atlanta for the steel magnate, Andrew Carnegie. Carnegie was well known for his support of worthy causes. But at the party, Martha found herself interrupted after exchanging only a brief greeting with Carnegie. She discovered his travel plans from an aide and drove, still in evening dress, to his train. The next morning, her finery somewhat wrinkled after sitting in it all night, she was able to breakfast with Carnegie, and she received permission to see him later in New York. Her mission completed, she left the train at Washington and boarded one headed for Georgia.

When later she met with Andrew Carnegie, her eloquent portrayal of the sad plight of the mountain people and of the positive benefits provided by her school persuaded him to promise a check for fifty thousand dollars — provided she could raise another fifty thousand within a few months' time.

It was hard going; after two weeks in New York, she had only four thousand dollars. Mr. Carnegie took a hand, insisting that a wealthy friend, Mrs. Russell Sage, add twenty-five thousand to the fund. Still, there was a long way to go.

Discouraged, she stumbled one day into a New York church. The minister spoke kindly to her and she told him how much she disliked asking people for money.

"Never think of yourself as a beggar. You are an ambassador of the King of kings," he reassured her.

She continued her work in the city, writing letters, tramping from meeting to meeting, and spending hours on the telephone. She became ill. Feverish, she nonetheless dragged herself out of bed one morning because she was to address the women's guild of a wealthy Manhattan church. Weak and dizzy, she spoke feelingly of the hard lot of the mountain people, beset by disease and malnutrition, yet always hospitable, intelligent, and responsive to sincere concern. She described her students and their eagerness to work for an education. She contrasted the lives of these descendants of early settlers with those of others, more fortunate, who had found a good life in the land of their dreams.

Miss Berry's eloquence was inspired by deeply rooted feelings. She finished her speech, turned toward her chair — and fainted. After she had been moved to an anteroom and brought to consciousness, the guild president came running into the room.

"Good news, Miss Berry! Our women have pledged the rest of the amount you need to reach your goal. Your endowment is secure."

Then at last Miss Berry returned home to Georgia for rest and for a post-Christmas celebration.

The list of interested donors to Miss Berry's school was becoming impressive. Most remained loyal supporters for life, and some left money in their wills. President Theodore Roosevelt was also interested in Miss Berry and her school. He invited her to the White House and introduced her to a group of influential persons. They too were impressed by what she was doing, and many of them gave generously to the school.

The president also brought up a point that Miss Berry had long had on her mind. "What about the mountain girls?" he asked. "What will happen to them as their brothers become educated?"

Over the objections of her board of trustees, Miss Berry soon was at work on a school for girls, to be located on the same property about a mile away. The trustees considered resigning — but stayed on. The girls' school opened on Thanksgiving Day in 1909. Their program included important homemaking skills, like meal planning, canning, and cleaning.

A few years later, in 1916, Miss Berry, again over the protests of her board, added a grammar school for the adult students who wished to receive the education denied them in their childhood. All students at the schools continued to work regularly on school projects; little outside help ever was necessary.

Miss Berry had worked out a dramatic plan for impressing visiting donors. If possible, she arranged for them to arrive at night. As they drove up from the railway station, the white gateway, inscribed "The Gate of Opportunity," swung open. Double lines of students marked the driveway; each held a lighted candle. The car lights were dimmed as the guests rode slowly through the pine forest to the reception hall, where they were officially welcomed. The visitors were also serenaded by candlelight, and when they left their last memory was the soft strains of the farewell song, "God Be With You Till We Meet Again."

Among the schools' most enthusiastic supporters were Henry Ford and his wife Clara. They gave impressive Gothic buildings for the girls' school, provided needed tractors, and even purchased a nearby brick factory for the school program. They approved of the hard work required of the students and were frequent visitors to the school.

In the 1920s, Miss Berry began to receive the fame she deserved. Many articles were written about her, and she received several medals and citations. The Georgia legislature in 1924 named her Distinguished Citizen of Georgia. The next year she was awarded the Theodore Roosevelt Memorial Medal for Distinguished

*The Ford dining hall on the Berry campus, completed in 1927*

Service. As he presented her with this award, President Calvin Coolidge said,

> In building out of nothing a great educational institution for the children of the mountains, you have contributed to our time one of its most creative achievements. Because of you, thousands have been released from the bondage of ignorance, and countless thousands of the generations to come will walk in light. . . .

The twenties and thirties continued to be busy years for Martha Berry. She traveled extensively, always talking about the schools and raising money. The Great Depression of the 1930s made fund raising difficult, but Miss Berry doubled her efforts and kept the schools going.

By the mid-thirties the schools became better off financially, and Martha could concentrate on administration, overseeing a student body of over twelve hundred. In 1926 the school had expanded into a junior college, and in 1930 it had become a four-year college. Her land acquisition program had added thousands of acres, and a continuing beautification plan made the campus one of the most beautiful in the country.

The work program was still a unique feature of the school. Perhaps the students were unique too. In a 1955 magazine article on Berry College, one professor remarked, "The students here don't throw up a wall of resistance and say 'teach me if you can.' They have worked out their tuition and they want to get the most out of it." Another teacher said, "They've got me working as I never have in thirty years of teaching."

From its earliest days the highlanders appreciated the school. An old mountain woman once walked ten miles to bring a basket of eggs. Miss Berry urged her to keep some for herself, but the woman's response was swift and direct:

"Miss Martha, I know what a time you-all are havin' at the school, and I want to help out what little I can. These eggs ain't much, but it's all I got, and I want you to have them. You've got to keep this school a-goin', 'cause tomorrow ain't never been touched."

Miss Berry summed up her life's philosophy when she responded to the presentation of the gold medal of the National Institute of Social Sciences, in 1939. She said,

"We walk from one place to another on the friendships we have made. And it is wonderful to be allowed to work; it is one of God's greatest gifts. It is a privilege to work for boys and girls you believe in; it keeps you going through all kinds of hardships."

"She thought anybody could do anything he tried to do," recalled Inez Henry, in *Miracle in the Mountains,* a book she helped write about Miss Berry. "Usually, she was right. Nobody dared say no to Miss Berry." Inez Henry was Miss Berry's long-time secretary.

The outbreak of World War II in Europe found Miss Berry in poor physical condition. In 1940, she was invited to Dallas to receive a salute from Variety Clubs of America as the American who that year had done the most for humanity. Her doctor declared that she was too ill to go. But Miss Berry, determined as ever, secretly took a plane from Atlanta. A roaring crowd of well-wishers at the Dallas airport led her in a street parade through the city. At the banquet that night, she spoke with inspiration and energy, explaining, "My doctor told me I couldn't make a long train trip, but he didn't say I couldn't fly! He told me I couldn't make a speech, but he didn't say I couldn't talk!"

Her poise and her enthusiasm for her cause made her the star in a room full of radio and theater stars.

But by her October birthday the following year, Miss Berry, now seventy-six, was confined to the hospital. On the night of February 26, 1942, Atlanta had its first blackout of the war. That same night, Miss Berry's light flickered too, and it quietly went out.

At dawn, the bell in Mount Berry's spired chapel began its mournful toll.

Visitors today to the Berry Schools, Mount Berry, Georgia, can enjoy a tour of Oak Hall and of the new Martha Berry Museum and Art Gallery, built next to the small log cabin of the founder's childhood.

The schools themselves have evolved into Berry Academy, an accredited college preparatory boarding and day school for boys and girls in grades six to twelve; and Berry College, a four-year accredited college including the liberal arts, sciences and professions, with graduate programs in education and business administration.

Scientific agriculture and forest management operations are maintained to afford practical experience for the future in these areas. Many students become teachers, or enter business or industry. Most of the students help finance their expenses through work.

The college and academy still stand for the balanced education Martha Berry emphasized when she selected the symbols on the Berry shield: a cabin — for simplicity; a Bible — for Christian principles; a lamp — for learning; and a plow — for labor.

*Patty Smith Hill worked to release the springs of creativity in the minds of kindergarten children.*

# "Checkerboard" Teaching

## PATTY SMITH HILL

*Pioneer of the modern kindergarten.*

Louisville, Kentucky, in the years following the Civil War, struggled bravely to recapture its former position as mistress of commerce in the South. Since the explorer LaSalle first glimpsed the beautiful falls on the Ohio River, back in 1670, the site had attracted many westward bound pioneers. Presbyterians, arriving with the Bible in one hand and a schoolbook in the other, were among the earliest settlers of the Gateway City. Their first church was built in 1816; some years later, their seminary was located there.

With the coming of the Civil War in 1861, however, the church split apart, dividing into southern and northern branches. The editor of the weekly *Presbyterian Herald,* a man named William Wallace Hill, was disturbed by the problems his church was having and decided to leave his job and accept a position as head of the Bellewood Female Seminary.

"Another daughter!" he exclaimed to his wife when Patty Smith Hill made her appearance on March 27, 1868. "I can see I am in the right line of work!"

Patty already had two sisters and one brother, and another sister and brother arrived during the next years.

The Hills were a lively and unusual family. They lived in the small village of Anchorage, a few miles from Louisville. Patty's parents were well educated and, for their time, quite progressive in their views. After graduating from high school, Mrs. Hill, then Martha Jane Smith, had been refused admission to all-male Centre College in Danville, Kentucky. Nevertheless, she had followed the entire course of study and passed the examinations, although the school would not grant her a degree.

The Hills had firm ideas about bringing up children. One of these ideas was that children should learn to handle tools. As soon as Patty was old enough to hold a hammer, she was set to pounding nails; soon she became skilled at carpentry. In the children's playroom the parents set up a variety of objects to inspire creativity: blocks, scissors, old magazines, empty spools, odd shoe strings, and a blackboard and chalk.

Each child in the family had a specific household task he or she had responsibility for. Also, the children were required to have a gardening project, in a special portion of the big yard. Patty chose beans and cucumbers for her plot one summer; later she added several hills of sweet potato plants. She liked them because the lush green vines were soon running all over the plot, reducing the amount of weeding necessary. And it was fun to dig the potatoes in the fall.

Thus encouraging both play and work, the Hills provided a happy childhood for their children. Moral lessons were taught by word and example, and the children were led to question what they read and heard before accepting it as truth.

Both parents were quick to reward a job well done with a kind word. Patty's special contribution to the Hill household became the care of the two youngest children. She had a knack for getting along with them, playing make-believe and other games, or marching to the beat of two pot lids banging together.

"Patty, you do have a way with children," Mrs. Hill often remarked.

"Oh, it's easy, Mama," answered Patty. "If they are making trouble, you just get their minds on something else. Same way if they start crying. Besides, I'd rather take care of them than mop floors or do the dishes!"

As she grew older, Patty joined her friends in town on daisy-picking outings with young men. Like them, she kept a floral album with pictures of flowers and humorous verses such as "Cows love pumpkins; pigs love squash. I love thee, I do, by gosh." Socials at the churches, opera night at the auditorium, and Wednesday night prayer meetings all provided chances for the young people to get together. But Mr. Hill had always suggested alternatives to early marriage.

"I'm not against marriage, don't misunderstand me," he would say in discussions around the family dinner table. "But I have seen too many women whose health broke down because of unhappy marriages — marriages they were forced into because they had no other choice. I hope, daughters, that you will never have to marry just to obtain a home. So you must prepare yourselves for a profession of some kind. Then you are not dependent on a man to supply your needs."

Patty adored her father and took his words to heart. In 1887 she was graduated from the Louisville Collegiate Institute, a private high school. Already she had made up her mind that the care of young children was to be her life's work.

Within two months of her graduation, an advertisement appeared in the *Courier-Journal*:

### A FREE KINDERGARTEN
Miss Bryan Returns to her Kentucky Home to Instruct Poor Children. She will also Train Young Teachers for Teaching. Celebrated System.

The next morning, Patty Hill knocked on Miss Bryan's door. After she had told Miss Bryan about her interest in young children and her experience with them, Miss Bryan began to describe what her kindergarten was going to be like. Kindergartens, she explained, were a fairly new idea in the United States. Almost all of them were based on the theories of Friedrich Froebel, a German philosopher and teacher. He was one of the first people to see the importance of schooling for very young children. He started a school in Germany in 1837, calling it a kindergarten, which means *children's garden*. Margaretha Schurz, a German immigrant, opened the first kindergarten in the United States in 1865. Others soon followed, but like Mrs. Schurz's, they were private ones, available to children whose parents could afford to pay a fee. Miss Bryan told Patty that the first free kindergarten, open to all children, had been started only fourteen years before. She herself had come to Louisville to bring that city free kindergarten education for the first time. Like the other private and free kindergartens, the Louisville kindergartens would be based on Froebel's ideas.

"Do you agree with Froebel's teachings?" Patty asked.

"I believe they have many good points, plus a worldwide reputation," responded Miss Bryan slowly. "And my kindergarten is opening under Froebel's banner. But I have some ideas of my own I would like to try out. And perhaps you will help me do so. We'll talk more about this in the future — for I would be very happy to train you in kindergarten teaching."

Patty Hill was one of Miss Bryan's first five students, and she was an immediate success in the kindergarten. Her love for children and her respect for them as individuals immediately won their hearts. Under Anna Bryan's direction, she organized her class according to Froebel guidelines.

Froebel believed that each child had a spiritual nature that needed to be uncovered. Education should be the process of unfoldment of the child's true self. Froebel was the first person to dare to say that a young child should spend most of his school time playing. Play, he believed, was the best way to encourage self-development. Kindergartens will always be in debt to Froebel for that idea.

Froebel's plan for kindergartens was a step-by-step program which was based on his concepts of "gifts" and "occupations." The gifts were divinely inspired to meet the needs of children, he claimed; they included balls, cubes, cylinders, and squares. The occupations, which offered the child ways to control and modify his materials, included activities like modeling figures from clay, lacing up strips of paper, and building forms with sticks. Occupations were used to increase understanding of the gifts. Froebel described in detail the program children should follow in kindergartens. Songs, games, stories, and poetry were included, and directions on how and when to use them were also given.

Dutifully Patty followed the instructions. And dutifully the children followed her instructions.

"My children get tired of making these little paper objects," complained Patty to Miss Bryan.

"Shhh!" said Miss Bryan, half seriously. "Don't let anybody hear you. Susan Blow, out in St. Louis, would throw you out of the kindergarten profession! Froebel's system is almost like a religion to kindergarten teachers in this country. They have been brought up on it, trained in it, and lectured about it for years."

But Miss Bryan agreed with Patty; she felt that Froebel's program was too "teacher-directed." It did not allow enough room for the child's own creativity. So they agreed to make a few changes in the Froebel program as an experiment.

Patty walked into her kindergarten the next morning with a head full of ideas.

"Here, children, are some paper dolls. One for each of you. Now, who would like to make a little doll bed for the doll to sleep in?"

Eagerly the children responded. They used Froebel's fourth "gift" — blocks — to make the beds. Some beds had high headboards, some had none; some were large, some small; some were cradles. Then the children pretended to give their dolls supper, sing them a lullaby, and put them to bed.

Patty was pleased to see the variety of ideas that resulted, and from that day on, she experimented with new ways of developing the children's creativity.

"Let's see what you can do with this clay," she might suggest. Instantly small hands were at work, changing the clay into objects of their own imagination, not into imitations of Froebel's imagination.

Both Patty and Miss Bryan were amazed at the

creativity and imagination their young charges showed. Even more impressive was the happiness of the children as they went about their own projects. It was amazing how little discipline they required.

Soon Patty was casting aside even the prescribed music and poems. One of her particular dislikes was a Froebel poem called "Clouds":

> In day-time clouds can see to float
>     In far-off skies of blue,
> But when night comes they are afraid
>     That they will tumble through.
>
> And so the angels tack them up
>     Between the sky's blue bars,
> Then when the golden nails shine bright,
>     We say, "Oh, see the stars!"

"What a false image that presents," Patty thought. "We aren't living in the first century. Our scientists know what clouds are, how the earth moves around the sun, how the light from the sun hides the stars in daytime. These children need to know facts. A correct view of the world is little enough preparation for the realities they will soon face." Out went "Clouds."

After a year of training under Miss Bryan, Patty was a full-fledged kindergarten teacher. And Miss Bryan asked her to direct one of the seven free kindergartens now established in Louisville. She and Miss Bryan continued working with new ideas for kindergarten teaching.

In 1890, Anna Bryan was invited to speak at the convention of the Education Association, a national group of educators. Her paper was entitled "The Letter Killeth." As Miss Bryan talked, Patty demonstrated with charts, showing how she led children to create their own activities. "We try to keep Froebel's spirit, that of the innate creativity of the child," explained Miss Bryan, "by allowing him to draw upon his own resources. But we think that keeping the letter of the law kills that spirit of creativity."

So impressive were her speech and Patty's demonstrations that visitors began to come to see for themselves what the Louisville kindergarten was doing. In just one year, three thousand of them appeared.

Anna Bryan left for Chicago in 1893 and became director of the Chicago Free Kindergarten Association. Patty Hill was put in charge of the Louisville Free Kindergarten Association, including the training school. She held this position until 1905. Patty's energy, her love of work, and her enthusiasm for her developing program were at a peak. And her kindergartens gained a national reputation for new ideas and practices.

Patty worked and studied constantly. "Every time I heard of a teacher who promised something different, I traveled to see him," she said later. She was especially influenced by two men who were leaders in modern educational thought: John Dewey and G. Stanley Hall.

When Patty began studying John Dewey's writings, she was so impressed that she went to Chicago to study with him as soon as she could. Dewey's ideas were very different from Froebel's. To him the rigid Froebellian program was the opposite of what children ought to have in school. Dewey believed that each child's activities should be directed by the child's own individual needs, not by the teacher. The child learned best by solving problems by himself. Patty began more and more to follow Dewey's concepts in her kindergarten.

In 1895, Patty was one of thirty-five kindergarten

teachers invited to attend a summer institute with G. Stanley Hall, a psychologist. Hall was studying how children developed both physically and mentally. This kind of study was a fairly new idea; up to that time teachers knew very little about how children developed. Hall's observations had shown that parts of the Froebel program were not well suited to children of kindergarten age. When he told this to his class, thirty-three of the thirty-five kindergarten teachers walked out of the room and left the summer course. The two that remained were Anna Bryan and Patty Smith Hill. Patty later described the summer in this way: "How exciting those weeks were! Professor Hall introduced us to the new child study movement, convincing us of the need to change materials, curricula, and methods. New knowledge about physical and mental health was breaking down the old ways of thinking."

The majority of the visitors to Miss Hill's kindergarten were impressed by her methods of teaching. The traditional Froebellians were becoming worried. A leader of this group was Susan Blow, who had established the first free kindergarten in the United States at St. Louis. Soon papers and articles in defense of Froebel's method, written by Miss Blow and her followers, were being presented at education meetings and were appearing in leading magazines and journals.

In 1893 the kindergarten teachers had withdrawn from the National Education Association, forming their own International Kindergarten Union. Within the IKU, a bitter battle was fought for twenty years between the progressives and the conservatives. The conservatives were the followers of Froebel; they saw his philosophy as a truth that should never be changed. The progressives, including Patty Smith Hill, argued for a scientific approach; they did not want a rigid kindergarten program, and they believed in observation and investigation. Encouraged by such thinkers as Dewey and Hall, the progressives carefully observed how children grew and how they learned. They also kept records of classroom incidents. They now could show, for example, that the large muscles of children developed earlier than the small muscles. Therefore, they said, large, bold play movements were proper for preschoolers, and finger muscles should be brought into regular use only after the child started first grade. These findings went against much of the Froebel program.

Miss Blow and the other conservatives, however, would not be convinced. "One man [Froebel] with the eyes of genius could see farther than any multiplication of observers," she insisted. The Froebellians were a powerful group. The debate in the IKU grew more and more bitter. In 1903, a committee of nineteen leading kindergarten teachers was established, whose goal was to come up with a clear statement about "contemporary kindergarten thought." This Committee of Nineteen, as it was called, reported to the field every year, outlining their areas of agreement and disagreement.

But in 1909 the differences among committee members became too great to be included in one report; three reports were written instead of one. The conservative report, written by Susan Blow, set forth Froebel's philosophy as the great truth for all kindergartens, and it supported the standardized kindergarten program designed by Froebel. The liberal report, written by Patty Smith Hill, expressed the new ideas. It argued for observation and for the study of child development, and it opposed any formal kindergarten program. The liberal report also included a generalized list of children's instincts and social needs known at the time. Most of them are still recognized today as valid for the age group studied. The third report, labeled the liberal-conservative report, attempted to blend Froebel's ideas with the new scientific ones.

Even though the conservatives argued long and well in support of Froebel, they gradually lost ground and eventually the liberal thinking took over. One of the events contributing to the decline of the Froebellian group was the appointment of Patty Smith Hill to the faculty of Teachers College at Columbia University. In 1905 Dean James Earl Russell invited Patty to lecture at the school, and then he made her a full-fledged faculty member. Before that time, the "kindergarteners" at Columbia had all been supporters of Froebel. James Russell decided to have Susan Blow and Patty Hill both give lectures to his student-teachers, and the two women did this from 1905 to 1909. Dean Russell later commented, "It is to the lasting credit of Patty Hill that she dared to meet the champion on her own ground and in fair combat won the victory."

Patty Smith Hill remained on the faculty of Columbia University Teachers College for thirty years, introducing to the student-teachers the procedures she had made famous in her Louisville kindergarten. And she went on to improve and develop further her ideas. Through trial and error, she established a comprehensive set of guidelines for the kindergarten classroom.

One of her contributions to kindergarten education was the introduction of many different kinds of toys, as well as tools, sandboxes, climbing gyms, and materials for science experiments. She developed a set of blocks (later named Patty Smith Hill blocks) that were large enough for the children to make a building they could walk into — whether it was a playhouse, a store, a post office, or a school.

Her kindergarten guidelines also stressed the spirit of self-government and cooperation. "We are practicing the principles of democracy here," she would explain. Because they were given many opportunities for learning from each other and from their own experiences, the children could begin to govern themselves. They then saw the teacher as guide and friend, not dictator.

As she introduced new learning situations to the children, Miss Hill always tried to teach with the idea of bringing about desirable changes in feeling, thinking, or acting. She emphasized social and moral concerns, such as sharing, cooperation, politeness, and respect for persons and materials.

Miss Hill was constantly interested in observing the children at play and keeping records of what happened in the classroom. She believed strongly that education should be based on what was learned by this observation. In 1923 the results of a five-year study at Columbia University's Horace Mann School were published in a book entitled *A Conduct Curriculum for the Kindergarten and First Grade*. This was the first of several books in a series on childhood education which she and her fellow teachers at Columbia wrote.

The many ideas and methods developed under Miss Hill's leadership during the first quarter of the century remain an important part of educational theory and practice to this day.

So the busy years flew by. The tall, vigorous woman was a tireless lecturer, spreading her philosophy through the country at numerous institutes and meetings, to students in all fields of early childhood education. She wrote a few articles, but she devoted most of her energies to speaking, demonstrating, and experimenting — always experimenting to discover better ways to achieve desired goals.

"Oh, the children, the children," she remarked in a 1927 interview. "How I wish I could be with them forever. They have taught me everything I know. Let me tell you a few things I have learned from them.

"In the early days, all the children were supposed to sit in a circle while you explained to them the topic of the day. I was looking first at one side and then at the other when little Howard broke in.

" 'Say, Teacher, who are you talking to, anyhow?'

"That is when I realized that in a circle you are not talking to anyone, just spraying ideas over a group of children. No more circles for me! By speaking to individuals or small groups, it is easy to get an exchange of ideas and discussion.

"And then again, while I was trying to work out ways of developing social consciousness, little Jack came to my rescue.

"A canary bird had been given the children and they crowded about his cage in much excitement. Jack said, 'What is his name?'

" 'He doesn't have a name,' I said.

" 'Then I will name him,' said Jack.

" 'But, Jack, does the bird belong to you?'

" 'No, he doesn't.'

" 'Who has the right to name him, then?'

" 'I suppose all the children ought to name him. . . . Miss Hill, please call the children together to name the bird.'

" 'But, Jack, you are the one who wants the bird named. Can't you call the children together?'

"Uncertain, but determined, five-year-old Jack

went from one group to another, saying, 'Let's name our bird right away.'

"Jack got Leland and Margaret and Sally to help arrange chairs in a circle. He took charge. He told everybody to be quiet while the little stutterer was giving his opinion. The bird was named.

"Jack taught us that the small, spontaneous group is the natural unit for work with little childen.

"In another instance, a group of six-year-olds showed that little children *do* have real purpose. They worked for a week on a model of a Fifth Avenue bus. They showed that youngsters can concentrate if the job is interesting.

"We wanted music to be creative. My sister Mildred invented a song, 'Happy Birthday to You.' It started out as 'Good Morning to You.' The tune has even been used in Broadway musicals. . . . We introduced all kinds of musical instruments: bells, triangles, horns, water glasses — anything to call attention to the beauty of sound. The beat of the music teaches rhythms to the children.

"We let the children make up their own plays. We substituted free drawing for mere copying of lines. Soon, psychologists were writing us for the children's pictures. They were astonished by the imagination, observation, and technique revealed by these babies."

Patty Smith Hill received numerous awards and much recognition for her pioneering work in the "new" kindergarten. Columbia University gave her an honorary doctorate. Educators throughout the country acknowledged that she had given children a new freedom, releasing them from the rigid control of adults in their early years of schooling.

Dr. Hill officially retired from Columbia University in 1935. She continued to work, however, as a volunteer at the Hilltop Community Center in New York. There she kept experimenting with new methods for training teachers. In all, she spent over forty years in the kindergarten, shaping it with loving, knowing hands. It was her life.

"It was a hard fight for each inch gained," she said of the early years, when creative play was a new idea. "We met opposition at every turn. At first, even in the experimental Horace Mann School, we had to call the kindergarten a playroom. . . . We kept records to prove that freedom did not mean disorder."

Summing up her years of experience as a teacher and a trainer of teachers, Dr. Hill said, "There are two great divisions of teachers — cookbook and checkerboard. By recipe, they spoon feed — the cookbook types. But can you figure out ahead of time your campaign on a checkerboard? The cookbook type skips the most vital factor: reaction of the other mind." Patty Hill was certainly one of the "checkerboard" teachers.

Dr. Hill's remarkable vitality ebbed slowly away; she died on May 24, 1946.

Today kindergartens are again being analyzed, and once more divisions are arising. Some think the main purpose of kindergartens should still be socialization — getting along with others. Some think that development of intellectual powers is the important goal. Perhaps there will be another Patty Smith Hill to mark the last quarter of the twentieth century. But it is unlikely that there will ever be another with such singleminded devotion to her charges. Her theme song, which she repeated often, rang out until the end:

"Children! Children! I wish I could stay in kindergarten with them forty years more."

*Florence Sabin, in her careers as professor of medicine and crusader for public health legislation, made a lasting impression in the field of medical education.*

# Passing It On

## FLORENCE SABIN

*Teacher of medical science, crusader for public health.*

"Now, Florence, we must do as Papa says," whispered nine-year-old Mary Sabin to her younger sister. "We must try hard not to cry."

Florence nodded, holding back the tears as she caught hold of her father's hand. Slowly the three of them walked behind the horse-drawn wagon carrying the body of Mrs. Sabin to the Denver cemetery.

Florence made herself look past the graveyard to the Rocky Mountains towering beyond. Out of the corner of her eye she saw the tiny mound, hardly a year old, of a baby brother's grave, next to the yawning hole that stood ready to receive her mother's rough pine coffin. A few words of prayer, and the simple service was over. The Sabin family walked sadly away.

When they reached home, they found Aunt Min in the kitchen fixing supper. "I am making enough biscuits to last you a few days," she announced. "And there is plenty of meat in the smokehouse. You can manage until your father finds a housekeeper. Mind, now, don't give your papa any trouble. Wish I could stay awhile longer to help. But I have little children at home, and now your little brother Albert to care for, too. So I'll be catching the next train home to Central City. Remember, you girls behave yourselves."

And giving them a hug and kiss, their kindhearted aunt bustled about, readying for her departure with their baby brother. Soon the little Sabin family, now just two girls and their father, were left alone. In a few days it was arranged for Florence, then seven years old, and Mary to enroll in Wolfe Hall, a private boarding school near Denver. Slowly they began to adjust to the many new changes in their young lives.

Mr. Sabin visited them at Wolfe Hall nearly every weekend, and sometimes he took them on trips to the city or to the nearby mountains. Once, they went to see their old home, perched on a cliff in Central City, Colorado, in which the girls had been born.

It was in 1860 that George Kimball Sabin had left his structured Vermont life to see what frontier existence in Colorado was like. At that time people were pouring into Colorado to make their fortunes in gold, and Central City was a real boom town. Although George Sabin had been in medical school in Vermont, he thought he would try to make his fortune first, and see the great wild west at the same time. Then in 1867, a young Vermont girl named Serena Miner arrived in Central City to teach school, and he fell in love with her. They were married in 1868, and Mary was born the following year. On November 9, 1871, Florence Rena Sabin made her appearance.

Now, as Mr. Sabin showed his girls around Central City, he described to them what the old mining days were like. "In those days, the area around Central City was called the richest square mile on earth. They had about four thousand miners, or prospectors, when I arrived. Most of them were sleeping in tents or on pine boughs.

"The work was pretty hard, too. Had to strip sand and dirt from the banks and shovel it into heavy pans or sluice boxes, running water over it to pan out the gold. Lots of folks couldn't make it. They had come out in wagons with big signs saying 'Pike's Peak or Bust.' Going home, their signs said 'Busted, by Gosh!' But I've managed to make a fair living out of the mines since I became a superintendent."

"Why did we move to Denver?" asked Mary.

"Because you were old enough to go to school," responded her father. "We liked Central City, though. Those were exciting days. The year after you were born, Florence, the Teller House was built — and a grand hotel it was. When President Ulysses Grant visited the next year, the miners laid down a pavement of silver bricks, worth twelve thousand dollars, so the president and his lady could walk from the stagecoach to the front door without muddying their feet! But the town was still pretty rough, and the schools in Denver are better, because it is the capital. Colorado only became a state in 1876, after all."

Many changes had come to George Sabin's life since those early days in Central City. The death of the first boy, then of Mrs. Sabin, were hard blows for him. Then baby Albert died when just a year old, and George Sabin was deeply saddened. Still, he had the two little girls to care for. He tried to be with them as much as possible.

But it was with a sense of relief that he one day read a letter from his brother Albert in Chicago. "Send the girls to us for awhile," he wrote. "They need to have some family life." The fall school term at Wolfe Hall had just begun, and Albert had realized how lonely his nieces must be.

Thus it came about that George Sabin took his neatly dressed daughters to the Denver railroad station and set them on the train to Chicago. As the train started up, cinders flew into their eyes, and soot dirtied their new dresses, but Mary and Florence were too excited to notice. The big locomotive up front belched fire and smoke as it puffed along with a roar; the cars lurched from side to side as the train rounded the numerous curves. On through the night it sped, through Omaha, past tiny towns no more than dots on the map, over mountains and along the great prairie. Finally, it deposited its passengers in the bustling metropolis of Chicago — soon to become known in such terms as hog butcher to the world, capital of the west, and railroad center of the universe.

Their uncle and aunt and their cousin Stewart, a year older than Mary, gave the girls a hearty welcome and the girls' visit lengthened to four years.

The years were pleasant ones. The girls especially enjoyed the evening songfests at their new home. After supper cousin Stewart would sit down at the piano, singing as he played. The others would quickly join in. At first Florence had been shy, just tapping her foot in time with the music, but soon she was singing too.

The girls also enjoyed exploring the big city in Uncle Albert's company. They were interested in the work being done to reverse the course of the Chicago River. In 1855, it had been decided to raise the city above the lake level, in some places as much as twelve feet. Canals were built, and the river was dredged for fill. By 1900, the river would finally be made to flow out of Lake Michigan rather than into it. This prevented the city's sewage from polluting the lake, which is the source of Chicago's drinking water.

"One of our citizens made a big reputation a few years ago," related Uncle Albert. "His name was George Pullman. He got together twelve hundred men and five thousand jackscrews, and raised the Tremont House Hotel eight feet, without disturbing a guest or cracking a cup!"

"Oh, I've heard of Mr. Pullman," said Mary. "He copied the bunks that miners use, to make sleeping berths on trains."

"That's right," said Uncle Albert. "They are called Pullman cars. He got his start right here in Chicago."

"Why is it always men who get things done?" inquired Florence. "I never hear of any women becoming famous."

"Well, there are a few in the history books. But usually women are busy taking care of houses, husbands, and children. And, besides, they don't take naturally to the business or professional world."

"Why?" persisted Florence. "What's the difference in their minds?"

Uncle Albert had no answer to Florence's question. And the subject was dropped.

Uncle Albert was a schoolteacher and had a library full of interesting books. Florence spent many happy hours reading behind a large chair, leaning against its back or sprawled out on the rug. One of her favorite books was a selection of fairy tales. Entranced, she was quickly lost in a world of fantasy, as dreams of princes and princesses swirled through her head.

The story of the ugly duckling, rejected by all

until his sudden transformation into a beautiful swan, made a special impression on Florence. She read it over and over again. And whenever a dream broke in two, she consoled herself with the thought: "Never mind. I'm just like the ugly duckling. Someday I will turn into a beautiful swan, a beautiful, graceful, white swan."

Uncle Albert saw to it that the children learned to enjoy music. In addition to the songfests at home, he took them to concerts and opera performances in the city. Florence loved the music and yearned to play the piano like her cousin. One day, she timidly asked Mr. Sabin, "Uncle Albert, do you think it would be possible for me to take piano lessons like Stewart? I know it costs money, and I will work extra hard to help pay for them. But I would so like to play the piano!"

"Why, bless my soul, I never thought of it. Of course you shall have piano lessons. I'll call about a teacher in the morning."

Florence was soon started on a musical career. Though her hands were quite small, she practiced conscientiously and learned quickly. In a few years she was playing so well that she began thinking of becoming a concert pianist.

The girls attended school in Chicago, and during the summer vacation they went to visit their Sabin grandparents in Vermont. They loved to take walks along the country roads after the chores were done, collecting wild flowers such as they had never seen before. Returning with large bouquets, they would ask "What's this? What's this?"

And Grandmother Sabin would answer patiently, "That's St. John's wort." Or, "Jewel-weed." Or, "Arethusa."

Grandmother Sabin was never at a loss when illness threatened. When she noticed how little supper Mary ate one night, she said, "Child, what ails you?"

"My throat hurts," replied Mary.

Immediately, Grandmother rose from her chair, hurried into the kitchen, and got a glass of water, to which she added a teaspoon of apple cider vinegar.

"Take this and gargle for three minutes," she said, "then swallow what's left. Do this every hour till bedtime."

By morning, Mary was well.

"Grandmother, you are a good doctor," remarked Florence. "Did you teach Papa how to doctor?"

"Maybe I influenced him," she replied. "It was a great disappointment to us that he never finished the course. And we do need doctors around here. If only you girls had been boys, you could have taken up medicine." She sighed.

"But aren't there any lady doctors?" asked Florence.

"Oh, no. It wouldn't be ladylike for women to be learning all those things doctors have to know. At least, I never heard of any women doctors."

But Grandmother Sabin was mistaken. Dr. Elizabeth Blackwell, in 1849, had become the first woman in the United States to receive the degree of doctor of medicine. Since then, a few more women in the United States had followed her example. Of them, Florence learned later.

"I would like to be a doctor," she told Grandmother. "Maybe I could learn enough so that people like my mother and my little brothers would not have to die so young."

After Florence and Mary had been with Uncle

Albert for four years, they were sent to Vermont again, this time to attend the Vermont Academy. Florence was nearly twelve. At first the girls stayed with their grandparents. Then, after the death of their grandmother, they became boarding students. Florence studied hard, and especially worked at her piano practice. One spring, she was chosen to play a piano solo at commencement exercises.

Mary was always the leader; Florence was content to walk in her shadow. Often, while Mary was off playing with her friends, Florence sat alone in her room, poring over her books or practicing the piano. So when Mary graduated and enrolled at Smith College in Massachusetts, Florence begged to stay in Chicago with Uncle Albert and his family. Kindhearted Albert Sabin gave in, but the following year he persuaded Florence to return to the academy for her senior year. To the surprise of nearly everyone, Florence was elected president of her class. She could hardly believe it.

"Are you sure? Do you really want me?" she exclaimed to the group who brought the news.

"Of course, Florence. You're just the girl for the job. We will always be proud that you were president of our class. You are the smartest girl we know!"

For many days Florence walked on a cloud of inward happiness. Was it possible the duckling was beginning to turn into a swan, she wondered. As she tried to concentrate on the Mozart sonata, her mind kept wandering to concert halls where a captivating Miss Sabin was bowing to applauding audiences shouting "Bravo! Encore! Encore!"

Rudely, the dream was shattered. As she practiced her piano one night after supper, a group of girls paused to listen.

"Play something besides those old Czerny exercises," begged one.

"Yes, Florence," chimed in another. "You may as well play something we like to hear, because you'll never be anything but an ordinary piano player. So skip the scales and give us a song."

Florence started a new piece, but her head bent lower to the keyboard. She continued to the end, but the tempo became slower and slower. At its end, she closed down the piano, got up without a word, and hurried out of the room.

Near the kitchen door stood an old elm tree. Through some early accident, one of its limbs had been bent into a natural seat. Florence had spent many lonely hours on that perch, away from prying eyes. Though the tree was now winter-bare, the little seat still gave her comfort. There Florence sat for a long while, studying her short, stubby hands and stretching her fingers to the utmost.

"It's true; I can barely reach an octave," she whispered to herself. "They will never grow any longer. Clara is right. I can never be a concert pianist."

Tears trickled down the young girl's face as she bade good-bye to her life's dream. Then she drew herself erect.

"I'll not settle for second-best, either. I'll just have to find another career. And I can do it! If my parents could be pioneers, so can I! Just you wait!"

Florence began studying harder than ever. She graduated with high honors, although, unfortunately, none of her family could come to her commencement.

The following year she joined Mary at Smith College, where the sociable Mary was well established and thoroughly enjoying the extracurricular activities.

Her friends tried to include Florence in their plans, and Florence's classmates were quick to admire her scholastic ability, but Florence would not come out of her little shell.

Mary was exasperated. "You have to make some effort yourself," she scolded. "I can't do everything for you!"

"Come on, Flo," she called one day. "Some of the Amherst College boys are coming over for a sociable. It ought to be fun."

She dragged Florence to her room, insisting that she put on her prettiest dress and brush down her flyaway hair. Grudgingly, Florence gave in, and then a feeling of excitement began to grow inside her. When Mary wasn't looking, she pinched her cheeks to give them color, and she began planning a conversation with the beau she was hoping to meet.

I'll say, "How do you do, sir? A lovely evening, is it not?"

And maybe he'll say, "Indeed it is, Miss Sabin, and I feel fortunate to be here."

And I'll say, "Tell me about your school; I understand that it is a fine place, with excellent professors."

And maybe he'll say, "Oh, let's not talk about school. Let's talk about more pleasant things — you, for example. Your accent indicates that you are not a native of Massachusetts."

And I'll say, "How clever of you to notice. Indeed, I come from Colorado. . . ."

"Florence! Come on!" Mary grabbed her sister's arm. "The party has already started. We must hurry."

Off the sisters ran to the reception hall. Proper introductions were made by a chaperone, and Mary was soon chatting away with a tall young man named

Thomas. His friend, James, politely addressed a remark to Florence.

"I understand you are in the freshman class. How do you like the school?"

"Fine," mumbled Florence.

"I do think freshmen have a terrible time, don't you? The upperclassmen order us around as if we were slaves! Is that the way it is at Smith?"

"No."

The young man tried again.

"How do you like our climate? Is there much snow in Colorado? Do you live near the Rockies?"

"Denver."

"Oh, Denver. That is the mile-high city, isn't it? I suppose our mountains seem pretty tame."

"Not at all," said Florence politely.

"Oh." The young man glanced around.

"Well, I think I had better speak to that old chaperone over there. She is glaring at me like a one-eyed dragon. But it has been nice talking to you. Excuse me."

"Thank you," responded Florence.

Looking around to be sure Mary was not watching, she walked unnoticed out of the hall, then fled to her own room. There she stood before the mirror, looking closely at the image it revealed.

"H-m-m. Frizzly hair. Snub nose. Round face. Ugly glasses. Squatty figure. Florence, my girl, you may as well face it. The world of romance might well pass you by. So it is up to you to plan your own life. What to do? Well, this is the time to decide. This is the time to make some plans." Then she went to bed.

She woke the following morning with new purpose and determination. Before the year was out, she had won a reputation for brilliance in her studies. The professors complimented her. Other students asked to borrow her notes. And though she and Mary still took long walks together, Florence began to be more independent of her sister. She was determined to chart her own life.

When Mary graduated, she returned to Denver to be a public school teacher, a position she held until her retirement many years later. Florence was now completely on her own.

But she had discovered the world of the sciences. The chemistry professor, Dr. Stoddard, introduced her to the laboratory. The excitement of experiment and discovery led her to spend extra hours in the lab, exploring the new world opened up by slide and microscope. Election to the Colloquium, a select group of science students, provided a needed social outlet to which Florence slowly responded. The club met every Saturday, either at Dr. Stoddard's home or in the lab, to discuss scientific problems or to describe their own experiments and theories. There was much lighthearted gaiety as the students poured tea from a glass beaker, or measured out sugar and cream in a test tube.

"Why, Florence, you talk like a professor!" exclaimed one of the girls one day, listening to Florence tell about her most recent experiment. "I didn't know you could be so eloquent!"

Indeed, as enthusiasm for her subject overcame her natural shyness, Florence's eyes began to sparkle, her face beamed with excitement, and her hands made graceful gestures. She began to feel more confidence in herself.

The college physician was a woman, well liked by the students. Florence knocked on her office door one morning and was warmly welcomed.

"I have been thinking about my plans after I

graduate in June," began Florence. "I wonder if it would be possible for me to be a doctor, like you."

"Well, Florence," began Dr. Preston, "of course it is possible. But it is a long, hard road. Men don't want women to be doctors, and patients don't want women for doctors. Even the professors sometimes make it harder for women. There are a thousand little problems and a few tremendous ones — such as finding a hospital that will allow you to intern after you have finished medical school. But if you have the determination — I know you have the intelligence — you can do it. Just be prepared to go that extra mile, every day."

"Oh, I will, I will!" exclaimed Florence. "I will work day and night. I will give up everything else, if only I can be a doctor. I know my father would like it more than anything in the world."

"Is your father a doctor?"

"No," said Florence. "He never finished medical school. I have always wanted to do it for him. Since I have done pretty well in my science courses, I believe I can pass the medical course. But first I must earn the money for it."

"Can't your family help you?"

"No, not financially. But I can teach for a few years, and then. . ."

"Well, Florence, it is too bad you can't go right ahead. There is a brand new medical school opening this very year at Johns Hopkins University in Baltimore. A group of women raised the money to get it started after the original funds proved unavailable. And they have insisted that women be admitted on the same basis as men. I believe it is the finest medical school in the country; at any rate, it has a brilliant faculty."

Florence's face fell; it was disappointing not to be

able to start right away. But immediately she brightened.

"Never mind. I'll get there in time. You have encouraged me to believe I can be accepted. Thank you very much, Doctor."

After graduating from Smith with honors, Florence left Northhampton in June to join her sister Mary in Denver. There she quickly found a teaching position in her old school, Wolfe Hall. When the term began in the fall, Florence was ready. Her friendly manner and enthusiastic approach to her subject, history, soon made her a popular teacher. She related the history course to current events, bringing in appropriate references to literature and social customs. Although she demanded excellence from her students, she also made sure they liked what they were doing.

"Old Flo's working us to death," they muttered to each other. But they worked.

Florence was surprised to discover that she was a good teacher and that she enjoyed teaching. But she never lost sight of her original goal.

Not content with the five-day school week, Florence organized nature walks on Saturday mornings for interested students, and she encouraged them to participate by promising a picnic at the end of the walk. From this volunteer effort came an unexpected dividend.

Impressed by her child's enthusiasm for the Saturday walks, a mother came one day to call on Miss Sabin. The following week, she invited Florence and Mary to spend the summer at her home on Lake Geneva in Michigan, teaching a nature class for her children and their cousins. The sisters were delighted to accept the invitation. They had a wonderful summer, and a lasting friendship developed between Ella Strong Denison and the Sabin sisters. In Denver, they were invited often to the lovely Denison home and enjoyed being in its gracious atmosphere. They caught a glimpse of a world quite different from any they had known before.

After two years at Wolfe Hall and another as an instructor at Smith College, Florence had saved enough money to enter medical school. At Johns Hopkins there were indeed a large number of women students completing the four-year course. Florence immediately found a hero and father-figure in her anatomy professor, Dr. Franklin Paine Mall. Her own father died during her second year of medical school.

Dr. Mall was a man of stimulating ideas. He soon found out what a hardworking student Florence was and began to encourage her research work. Florence felt much more at home in the laboratory than in the "Hen Pen," as the women's dormitory was called. In her senior year, Florence made a three-dimensional model of the brain and brain stem, from slides of a baby's brain. This project had never been done before. Florence's model was so good that copies of it were used in medical schools all over the country.

During their final year of medical school, the students did much practical hospital work. Florence found that she did not enjoy the pressure of constant medical rounds and everyday routines. "I'm always writing up physicals and lab reports, it seems," she wrote Mary. "Examine, write, then write some more. I never get time to do research."

She and another woman, however, found time enough to rank third and fourth in their class academically, thereby posing a problem for the faculty: the four Johns Hopkins hospital internships in medicine automatically went to the class leaders. But two of them to two women? Impossible! However, the group of Baltimore women giving the school financial support kept a close watch on their women students. There was no way out. And so Florence became an intern; it was a real breakthrough for women doctors at Johns Hopkins. But it was a hard year; many of the men did all they could to make things unpleasant.

"I can never be a regular doctor," Florence decided. "It is too nerve-racking. I want to go into research, where life can be quieter and more controlled."

To her great joy, the university gave her just the chance she wanted. After completing her internship, Dr. Sabin was offered a fellowship from Johns Hopkins for a research project. She spent a year in the laboratory, making important discoveries about the origin of the lymphatic vessels, which carry an important fluid known as "lymph" to body cells. For her first two papers on the lymph studies, she won a thousand-dollar prize. After this year of research, Florence was invited to become a member of the Johns Hopkins medical faculty, the first woman in such a position in the history of medicine. Florence accepted immediately. She had enjoyed her earlier teaching experience; now she could combine both research and teaching.

Then she went to Dr. Mall. "Please give me some hints on effective teaching," she said. "You are the best I know."

"Be careful not to make your teaching so rigid, Florence, that you rob your students of the pleasure of discovering things for themselves," he counseled. "It is important to make those first-year students happy about their choice of medicine. Keep them interested."

The Florence Sabin who met her first class in anatomy that summer day in 1902 was a far different person from the shy woman who started teaching history at Wolfe Hall nine years before. Success in medical school, especially in the laboratory, had given her assurance. Her lectures were delivered with sparkling eyes and vibrant voice, but she demanded hard work and concentration.

"Dr. Sabin," complained one of the young men, "you talk so fast, I can't keep up with my notes."

"Don't try," advised Dr. Sabin. "You are not supposed to take notes on my lectures — the facts are all in the textbook. Just jot down an idea or two; then, when you sit down to think about them, you can expand your thoughts."

Though she was demanding, "Aunt Flossie" was also sympathetic and understanding. She tried to communicate to her students her intense feeling for her work.

"Here, let me sit by you," she would say to a student peering through a microscope. "Look! Look hard at that blood cell. In it is the mystery of life. And we must decipher it!"

"I felt as if she were lending me her own eyes!" declared one of her students.

Nor did she spare herself. For a final examination in histology (the study of the microscopic structure of animal and plant tissues), she had one question: Identify all the tissues included in this stained cross section of the belly of a mouse. To make each cross section, she had taken out the intestines of a mouse, cut them up, mixed the fragments, stuffed them back into the body cavity, and had the sections cut. Then she had to judge and grade the reports of all eighty students.

One of Dr. Sabin's most valuable contributions to the teaching profession was her insistence on using living tissue to study body functions. She provided a new technique for studying blood cells which demonstrated the properties of living cells.

"We must watch the living cells, both normal and abnormal," she lectured. "Then we can see how each cell type responds to the demands of the body."

Probably the most memorable moment in her life, Dr. Sabin often said, was "when I was able to watch life begin. I saw the birth of the blood stream in a chick embryo. First, I watched the blood vessels form; then, the beginning of cells which differentiate into the red and white cells; and finally, the actual beginning of the heart with its first beat."

Not for Dr. Sabin the lazy life of a professor who drones on from the same notes year after year. After each lecture, she threw away her notes so that she could make a new approach the following year. And her enthusiasm for her subject impressed even the most negative of students.

"We used to pass her door on tiptoe," recalled one, "so that we would not disturb her laboratory quiet, for we knew that exciting things were going on in there."

Dr. Sabin did not ignore her students outside the laboratory or classroom. After each phase of study, she and her students held a big celebration. Once, after the section on brains was completed, the entire class went down to the basement. There, all the hundreds of dime-store plates used in the lab for staining cross sections were set up at the end of the room and the students took turns using them for target practice.

There were frequent suppers in her apartment for students and their friends. She often added musicians, writers, or painters to the guest list. Each person was assigned a job: setting the table, cooking, or washing the dishes. Dr. Sabin herself always supervised the broiling of the steak. With stop watch in hand, she counted off exactly three minutes . . . turn . . . three minutes more.

"A rare steak for rare persons," she said.

Dr. Sabin always believed that almost anything could be accomplished by hard work. She held her students to a high standard. To their own surprise, they often ended up achieving more than they thought themselves capable of. One of Dr. Mall's German professors once explained that his motto for teaching was: "Pass it on." Dr. Mall had followed this faithfully, and Florence Sabin also adopted it as her own.

"What you know to be true, tell others," she advised. "But accept nothing on faith. If the answer is easy, doubt it! Try to get as close as possible to the truth — but don't expect to find it. It is not an easy road, but it is an interesting one. The laboratory is as wide as the world. The choices for study are infinite. For instance. . ." and she would launch into a description of her study of the reaction of body cells to disease.

Many of her students did go into research, making notable contributions to the science of medicine. All helped spread the word that she was a superb teacher. Every medical student at Johns Hopkins between 1902 and 1925 took her anatomy class and benefited from the inspirational teaching that influenced literally thousands of persons.

Dr. Sabin did not completely confine her interests to the medical world. She recognized her role as a pioneer for the rights of women. She named her first car, an air-cooled Franklin, for the famous suffragette Susan B. Anthony. One of her close friends, Edith Hooker, was a leader in the movement to get the vote for women, and Florence often lent a hand in publishing the Maryland *Suffrage News,* or the *Equal Rights* magazine of the National Women's Party. She wrote letters to legislators. And she rejoiced with her Baltimore friends when in 1920 the Nineteenth Amendment, which gave women the vote, finally was ratified.

Dr. Sabin also took time to do volunteer work at the Evening Dispensary for Working Women and Girls. The dispensary had been organized by two other women doctors to provide better health care for Baltimore women. Its study of deaths from tuberculosis laid the foundation for the formation of the National Tuberculosis Association.

Suddenly, a crisis loomed in the ordered life of Florence Sabin. In 1917 Dr. Mall died. His position as head of the anatomy department went not to Dr. Sabin, who was next in line, but to a man. Not only for herself but for the cause of women's rights, Dr. Sabin was deeply hurt. Baltimore women protested and students petitioned, but in vain. Dr. Sabin wrestled with her feelings, conquered them, and quietly accepted a promotion to the post of professor of histology instead. This in itself was another first for a woman, the first time a woman had been given a full professorship at Johns Hopkins. For seven more years she continued to teach.

Her fame spread. Smith College awarded her an honorary degree, the first of fifteen she eventually received. In 1923 the National League of Women Voters named her one of the twelve greatest living American women. Two years before, she had delivered the opening address at Peking Union Medical College in China. Her election as a life member of the National Academy of Science in 1924 brought new progress to the struggle for equal rights, and distinction to her university.

The results of her basic cellular studies at Johns Hopkins were noted with increasing interest by Dr. Simon Flexner, director of the famous Rockefeller Institute for Medical Research in New York City. He invited Dr. Sabin to join his staff. If she accepted, she would be the first woman ever admitted to full membership in the Rockefeller Institute.

The decision was difficult.

"Here I am, a middle-aged woman, asked to leave my home of nearly thirty years, my friends, my students, my work," Florence debated with herself. "On the other hand, I can advance no further at Johns Hopkins; the limitless funds at the institute will mean that I can dictate my own future. With my own staff, I believe I can make a real contribution to the field."

In the end, she made the move. Soon she was enthusiastically at work with a carefully chosen staff, teaching her research associates, just as she had taught her medical students, the long, painstaking procedures demanded by the search for scientific truth. She stayed at the institute for nearly fourteen years.

Dr. Flexner was impressed with her work. "Her success was not scientific only," he said. "It was something more. She never ceased being a teacher, and she not only inspired young men to work at scientific problems, but she imbued them with high ideals of achievement. No one, I suspect, of her pupils left her without carrying away a sense of her rare generosity and her valuation of honest work."

In 1938, when she was sixty-seven, Dr. Sabin retired from the institute. She returned to Colorado to live with her sister Mary. For the next few years she traveled, gave speeches at various organizations, and did a research project back at the Rockefeller Institute. Then, near the end of World War II, she found herself appointed to a postwar planning committee on public health. A new career suddenly began for her. She worked on the project with the energy of a crusader. First she investigated existing health conditions in Colorado, finding them very poor. There were no up-to-date health laws, and the facilities for fighting disease were inadequate. Sewage pollution was common, milk production was unregulated, and the state's death rate was much higher than the national average.

She decided that the next step was to educate Colorado's citizens. In good weather and bad, she traveled the state, explaining to all who would listen the low quality of Colorado's health facilities and the means to improve them. Almost singlehandedly she got the legislature to pass meaningful laws on health in 1947. For her work, she was named by Colorado to the national Hall of Fame, and she received many more citations and awards. Two years later she was appointed manager of Denver's public health department, a post she held for three years.

At a birthday celebration, Dr. Albert Cohn, from the Rockefeller Institute, wrote to her: "Having led several lives, each of singular distinction, . . . how came you to possess these many skills and virtues? It has been, I think, because of your great humanity. You have cared deeply for your kind. And men have come to recognize in you that rare total person — of wisdom and of sentiment — heart and mind in just and balanced union."

"You know, Florence," remarked Mary one evening as they set out to visit a friend, "when Leon

Gordon painted that portrait of you a few years ago, I thought he was flattering you, making you look so beautiful. But now I'm beginning to think he did not do you justice. You have a kind of serenity that radiates goodness; it makes you look really beautiful."

Florence laughed. "Too late now!" she said. "I used to wonder if I would turn into a beautiful swan — but I never thought it would take fifty years! But you know, Mary, if I had had all that beauty I so desired at eighteen, I probably would have married some dull old miner and missed the marvelously exciting years I have enjoyed — and am still enjoying. But come on. We must make this a quick visit, so we can get home before the baseball game begins. Those Orioles have been my favorites for a long time, and I can't desert them now."

In the early 1950s, Dr. Sabin had received many more honors. One was especially meaningful. A new wing in the University of Colorado Medical School was named the Florence R. Sabin Building for Research in Cellular Biology.

By 1953, Dr. Sabin was having problems with her health. But her interest in science, reading, and baseball were as high as ever. She sat listening to the game that October 3, happy because her team was winning. As the seventh inning stretch was announced, she got up to walk across the room. Suddenly, her heart gave out and she dropped to the floor, dead.

Full of years and honors, Dr. Florence Sabin carried in her heart to the end the welfare of others, especially of women and young people. To them she left a legacy of courage, imagination, and wisdom. And to them her life says today, "Pass it on."

*Mary McLeod Bethune, founder of Bethune-Cookman College, worked tirelessly for the education of black Americans.*

# I Leave You Love

## MARY MC LEOD BETHUNE

*Tireless worker for education of black Americans.*

A lusty cry issued from the tiny black baby as the midwife gave her a brisk slap on the back.

"She shore is ugly!" she remarked, holding the wailing infant for the mother to see. It was July 10, 1875.

"No matter! She is born free! Mary Jane's been born free!"

Fourteen other children of Patsy and Sam McLeod had arrived before the Civil War brought freedom to the American blacks. After the war, the McLeods had managed to "work out" enough money to buy five acres of land from Owner McLeod and had adopted his last name. Then they had built for themselves a four-room cabin with a large fireplace, near Mayesville, South Carolina. Later they increased their holdings to thirty-five acres.

Grandmother Sophie, who lived with them, helped look after the children. She also passed on to them her strong faith in God. "Come on, children, it's time for prayers," she called out, morning and evening. To her,

God was a living person and she lived on terms of easy familiarity with Him, talking to Him all day.

As Mary Jane grew up, her father would sometimes take her with him to Mayesville, and she would see the fine homes of white people, with real glass in the windows. She wondered at the little girls in frilly clothes, white gloves, and soft shoes.

Mary Jane's mother did the washing for a white family, and Mary Jane often helped her with the work. Sometimes she was given an outgrown dress or two. One Saturday morning, on a trip to return a basket of clothes, Mary Jane was standing silently while her mother talked with the mistress of the house. A small child ran up with a book in her hand, and finding her mother busy, she turned to Mary Jane.

"Read me this story, Mary Jane," she said.

Her older sister snatched the book away. *"She can't read!"* she said scornfully.

On the way home, Mary Jane pulled at her mother's dress, saying, "I want to learn to read!"

Patsy McLeod glanced down at the earnest face.

"Ain't no schools for coloreds around here," she answered. "But — the teacher and the school will come. The Lord will send them." She felt that of all her children, Mary Jane most deserved to go to school.

The sight of that book had made a deep impression on Mary Jane. She could not get it out of her mind. *Reading.* She dreamed of it in spring while she dropped cotton seeds in the straight furrows plowed by her pa. Chopping weeds from the sturdy plants during summer's long hot days, she held it in her thought.

"Mary's as strong as an ox," her neighbors would say. "And smart, too, in spite of being so homely."

"Mary has a risin' soul," said her mother proudly.

"She will either go far or break her heart."

Mary knew she would go far.

"I had a vision," she said many years later. "Working in the fields as a child, I had a vision in which I saw buildings with wide open doors and people finding themselves welcome inside. I believed it would come to pass. For I had faith in *me,* like a deep river."

Early September was devoted to getting ready for cotton picking. All the fertilizer bags left from spring were washed and dried, ready for use as pick-sacks. Cutting off a broad piece for the shoulder strap, Mary then turned back the sack top several inches, putting a green cotton boll in each corner. Around these she tied a knot with the strap, adjusting it to bring the sack to her waistline.

Black skin glistening with perspiration, the McLeod family bent over the green stalks, plucking out the fluffy bolls and tossing them into the sacks. Mary Jane could pick 250 pounds of cotton a day. Large baskets stood at the ends of the rows to receive the cotton, and at the end of the day the filled wagon was taken to Cooper's gin for weighing.

The October sun was still summer hot, and the pickers made frequent trips to the gourds filled with cool water, lying under a tree. Mary tried to waste as little time as possible on these trips.

One morning a shadow fell across her sack. Quickly, she looked up. "Good morning," said a tall black woman. "I am Miss Wilson, from the American Presbyterian Church. I am going to start a school downtown. Would you like to come?"

Mary could only stare. But her mother, working nearby, fell on her knees and raised her hands to heaven.

"Thank you, Lord!" she cried. "Thank you!"

"Yes, ma'am," she then said to Miss Wilson. "She'll come. Mary is going to read at last!"

Early on the following Monday, Mary set out for school. She had on a stiffly starched gingham dress, heavy shoes with brass tips, and half a dozen little ribbons in her braided hair. Running most of the way, she covered the three miles long before Miss Wilson rang the bell.

Miss Wilson divided the room into sections. After a song, a Bible lesson, and a prayer, she wrote the letters of the alphabet on the black cardboard. Mary learned them all by heart before the day was over. She learned to write her name, too, copying it over and over on her slate. When school was out, Mary ran home as fast as she could. Gasping for breath, she cried out, "I can read, Granny, I can read!"

And soon she could indeed read, write, and use numbers. She tried to teach her brothers and sisters to read; she read the Bible to Granny. She began to help her father and other farmers with their accounts and their cotton weighing. They soon grew to respect her knowledge and abilities.

Six years passed swiftly by. Mary was ready to graduate from Mayesville Institute. She had a new white dress, and white stockings and shoes. How proud the McLeod family was! Mary's eyes were aglow as she received the congratulations of family and friends. But as she neared home, she wondered sadly if this was to be the end of her schooling. She was fifteen years old, almost a woman, but the future seemed dark. There was no high school for black students within three hundred miles.

Through the hot summer, she worked again as a

farm girl. Sometimes at night she would awaken, listening to the mournful whistle of the freight train lumbering through the sleepy little village.

"How can I get on that train?" she would wonder. And she would pray, "Thank you, God, for what you have already done for me. But, God, you said it in your own Book: 'For God so loved the world . . . that whosoever believeth in Him should not perish. . . .' Whosoever! That means a Negro girl has as much chance as anybody. I want that chance, God!"

Mary's prayers were answered sooner than she dared expect. One morning Miss Wilson appeared at the farm.

"Oh, Mary," she exclaimed, "God has answered our prayers. You can go to school again."

"Hallelujah! Hallelujah!" shouted Mary.

"Yes," continued Miss Wilson, "a Quaker lady out in Denver, Colorado, is giving a scholarship at Scotia Seminary in North Carolina. A scholarship to you. Her name is Miss Mary Chrissman. You will be able to finish high school."

"Oh, thank you, thank you, Miss Wilson." Mary danced up and down with joy.

At last the great day came. Though farmers in 1888 had little money to spend, friends and family had knitted and sewn with loving care an adequate wardrobe for Mary. She had packed the clothes carefully in a small bag. At the station, Mary walked up and down the tracks, straining eyes and ears for sign of the train. Finally it appeared, spreading black cinders far and near, and ground to a halt with the passenger coach precisely at the station door. Waving a last good-bye, Mary climbed on the train.

Time passed swiftly. Mary watched the fields flash

by, noting the poor condition of the cotton, still being picked though the price was less than nine cents a pound. Late in the afternoon, the conductor came through the coach, calling, "Con - - - cord! Concord, North Carolina! All out for Concord!"

Hastily, Mary retrieved her suitcase. She stepped from the train, looking anxiously about her.

Immediately, a white woman approached her. "Are you Mary McLeod?" she asked.

Mary nodded shyly, amazed that the woman was white. She was to discover that many of the teachers at Scotia were white — missionary ladies from the north who wanted to bring education to the blacks of the south.

Silently she followed her guide to the seminary campus. Inside Graves Hall, she laid her bag on the floor, admiring the sweeping staircase to the upper floors. Then, for the first time in her life, she climbed a flight of stairs. Mary was sure they led straight to heaven, and her musical soul provided a mute accompaniment to her steps:

> We are climbing
> Jacob's ladder,
> Soldiers of the Cross.
> Every step leads
> Higher, higher,
> Soldiers of the Cross.

Glories of glories! In her room were two beds, one for herself alone and one for her roommate. Having only two people in a room was new to Mary. In a few days, Mary had learned how to place a napkin in her lap, how to use a fork instead of just a spoon, and how to make the bed with beautiful crisp sheets.

As she watched black and white teachers eating together, Mary McLeod realized for the first time that racial equality was not an impossibility. In the back of her mind began to grow a dream.

Quickly she slipped into the routine of school life, her natural capacity for leadership soon showing itself. She was not an enthusiastic student of the liberal arts courses. She thought that she needed only a working knowledge of reading, writing, and arithmetic. It was more important, just then, to learn how to keep a house neat and clean, how to cook nutritious foods, and how to improve sanitary conditions, so she could teach her people. But she soaked up learning, both in books and without. The music teachers discovered that Mary had a clear, powerful contralto voice. Training her in the school choir, they soon had her singing solos in church.

During the six years at Scotia, the dream grew in Mary's heart: I must do something to help my people.

One night, she heard a sermon about the need for missionaries in Africa. The preacher told wonderful stories about the people there, some of them no doubt her own ancestors.

Mary took her dream to the principal, Dr. Satterfield. With his help, she composed an application to the Moody Bible Institute in Chicago. She was accepted, and Miss Chrissman again volunteered to pay her tuition for the year's course. Mary was ecstatic.

After graduation from Scotia, Mary went home to Mayesville. It was the summer of 1894. Tactfully, she tried to pass on some of the things she had learned at school. Her relationships with her parents and her grandmother deepened. More than ever, she appreciated their pride in themselves and in her, their faith in God, and their willingness to work hard. Later, she said, "I was shown goodness in my childhood. My parents believed in me. I learned to believe in other people."

A few short weeks and it was time for the trip to Chicago. When she boarded the train this time, she was ordered to the baggage car, where a part was reserved for "coloreds." During her stay at Scotia, changes had come to South Carolina. The white people were determined to regain power lost during the Reconstruction period after the Civil War. They passed laws separating blacks from whites in almost every aspect of life. So Mary McLeod, well dressed, clean, and neat, was shunted into the "colored" coach. From such experiences she formed a resolution she later expressed in these words:

> We must challenge, skillfully but resolutely, every sign of restriction or limitation on our full American citizenship. . . . We must challenge everywhere the principle and practice of enforced racial segregation. Whenever one has the price or can fill the requirements for any privilege which is open to the entire public, that privilege must not be restricted on account of race.

Arriving at Moody, Mary discovered that she was the only Negro American in the student body, though there were Africans, Chinese, Japanese, and East Indian students. Their common goal served to subdue any racial feelings.

"We learned to look upon a man as a man, not as a Caucasian or a Negro," she later recalled. "My heart had been somewhat hardened. As the whites had meted out to me, I was disposed to measure to them, but here, under this benign influence, a love for the whole human family, regardless of creed, class or color, entered my soul and remains with me, thank God, to this day."

Mary's musical talent earned for her a place in the choral group at Moody and gave her a special extra in her missionary work among the poor, the lonely, and the imprisoned. Field service, as this work was called, was a valuable part of the institute's training.

Mary's own faith needed renewing at times. Though Miss Chrissman's scholarship paid her tuition, there was no money to spare for extras. When she received the news that the family home had burned down, Mary could not help crying. Pa had to take out a new mortgage on the crop so he could build another cabin.

The very next day after she heard the news, some women invited her to sing for a large gathering in the city. Several days later, she received a brief note of appreciation and a check for forty dollars. Mary could hardly believe her eyes. Immediately, she mailed it to her parents. In 1895, forty dollars was a fortune to a black farmer in South Carolina, where cotton was selling for less than five cents a pound.

Just before commencement day, a blow fell. She had applied to the Presbyterian Mission Board for assignment somewhere in Africa, but she now received word that she had been rejected. There was no opening at that time for a black missionary in Africa.

Poor Mary! Her hopes were wrecked. Sadly, she went home. But she was learning how to cope with defeat. "When the Lord says no to me, I look into my head and search my motives," she explained later. "At Moody, I saw that part of my wanting to go to Africa was a desire for travel. So I went back home to teach school. With my first earnings, I paid off my father's mortgage."

A hundred miles or so from Mayesville, just across the Savannah River, which divides South Carolina and Georgia, lies the city of Augusta, aristocratic and old. Deep in its Negro section stood Haines Institute, a school founded by Lucy Laney, a black woman with unusual cultural attainments for her day. In her school, she emphasized not only the three Rs, but also art, music, and black history.

Here Mary McLeod taught for two years. She became even more convinced that practical training must go hand in hand with academic work. She began to think about starting a school of her own.

Transferring to the Kindell Institute in Sumter, South Carolina, Mary met a pleasing young man with a fine tenor voice, Albertus Bethune. He was teaching at Kindell too. Music gave them a common bond, and they fell in love. Not long afterwards, they were married in a Presbyterian church and Mary Jane McLeod became Mrs. Albertus Bethune. She liked the sound of her new name: Mary McLeod Bethune.

The young couple soon moved to Savannah, where Albertus had a teaching job. There, on February 3, 1899, Albert McLeod Bethune was born, ninetieth grandchild to Patsy and Sam McLeod.

Though the country as a whole had become quite prosperous at the turn of the century, living conditions for blacks had changed hardly at all. "What future is there for my people, for my son, if we don't get more education?" Mary Bethune often asked herself.

One night she had a vivid dream. She saw herself in a large body of water making her way to a faraway shore. The dream moved her to action. "It's like God telling me to go," she told Albertus. "I know He wants me to start my school."

Albertus was not encouraging. It seemed impossible to him that Mary could start a school with a nine-month-old baby to care for. But Mary was determined to find a way.

First she went to Palatka, Florida, to reorganize a little Presbyterian school there. She expanded her efforts into the community, holding afternoon Sunday school classes, visiting prisoners in jail, visiting the lumber and turpentine camps. Conditions in the camps were especially bad. Black people lived there in extreme poverty, and they had little hope for a better life. Mary's religious faith and her insistence on moral conduct, cleanliness, and hard work were greatly needed. But soon she felt the call to go farther south to Daytona Beach. The Florida East Coast Railway was under construction. Daytona was a major junction point, and many black railway workers lived there with their families. But Daytona Beach was also a winter resort for wealthy Northerners. Mary Bethune knew that she would need their financial help.

So, early one morning, she and her young son headed for the railroad station. After paying for her ticket to Daytona, she had only a dollar and a half left. When they arrived, she cheerfully set out to find the house of a friend of a friend.

Mrs. Warren welcomed her, listening with interest as Mrs. Bethune explained her mission. She enrolled her three little girls at once. Soon she introduced Mrs. Bethune to John Williams, who owned a two-story house near the railroad. Somewhat astonished, he heard himself agreeing to move, to put out his renters, and to rent his house to a total stranger for eleven dollars a month! Her dollar and a half provided the down payment. Mrs. Bethune had a school building.

When it was time for the school to open, six children were enrolled. Tuition was fifty cents a week. Pencils were made from charcoal, ink from elderberries. The city dump provided cracked dishes, broken chairs, and packing cases for desks.

The grand opening of the Daytona Literary and Industrial School for Training Negro Girls took place on October 4, 1904. The ABCs were combined with cooking and housekeeping lessons. An old sewing machine transformed gunny sacks into pillow cases and dish cloths. Dried Spanish moss, stuffed into a ticking, made a fine mattress for the rusty double bed, and two boarding students could be taken in.

"Cease to be a drudge; begin to be an artist,"

*An early building of the Bethune Institute*

wrote Mary McLeod Bethune on the cardboard blackboard.

The school grew, but finances were always a problem. Mary found many ways to help raise money. Albertus had now joined Mary in Daytona, and he sang with her in a quartet at local functions. Mrs. Bethune organized the little girls into singing groups, dressing them neatly in blouses and skirts. They sang on street corners and at parties.

In two years, Mrs. Bethune's school boasted two hundred and fifty pupils. She hired a young Hunter College graduate, Miss Frances Keyser, promising her challenge, not cash. Miss Keyser took charge of the curriculum, leaving Mrs. Bethune free to drum up support in an increasing variety of places.

One day she took another look at the dump heap that had supplied the chairs and desks when the school opened. She saw it in a different light this time. A campus! Looking up the owner, she asked if he would sell her the property.

"That smelly place for a school?" he asked in amazement. "Are you sure you know what you are doing?"

"I don't see a smelly dump heap," she replied earnestly. "I see thousands of boys and girls walking through open doors."

The man agreed to sell the property for two hundred dollars, with five dollars as down payment. At the moment, Mrs. Bethune did not even have the five dollars, but she promised to bring it soon. To raise the money for the land, she staged coffee parties, sold ice cream and sweet potato pies to construction crews, and knocked at doors asking for donations.

Once the down payment was made, she set her

pupils to work on the dump. Slowly the mound was leveled and low places filled in.

The Palmetto Club, an organization of socially concerned white women, became interested in her work. Some members agreed to serve on an advisory board, but suggested that having some men serve as trustees would be valuable too.

Boldly, Mrs. Bethune wrote a note to James M. Gamble of the Proctor and Gamble Company, asking for an opportunity to explain her school to him. He agreed to an appointment, and she persuaded him to visit the school.

When Mr. Gamble made his promised visit, he was accompanied by the mayor, a prominent realtor, and two black ministers. The little girls entertained the visitors with recitations and singing; then Mrs. Bethune told the story of her life. Simple but dramatic, her testament of faith deeply impressed her distinguished visitors.

At the end of her speech, she said, "Gentlemen, I want you to be trustees of a dream. A dream that is in my mind, in my soul. This" — and her arms swept over the scene — "is only the seed. It must grow into a great tree. Will you help?"

"Gladly," said Mr. Gamble. "I am honored."

The others echoed his words. Thus a board of trustees was formed. After they had left, Mrs. Bethune called the students to her side, offering a prayer of thanksgiving.

With renewed enthusiasm, Mrs. Bethune set out to get her new school built. Parents of her students donated their time and talents as carpenters, well diggers, brickmasons, plasterers, and mechanics. In a next-to-new, fifteen-dollar buggy, she drove around the city, begging discarded bricks, sand, and pieces of lumber. She insisted that the building plans include inside plumbing for three bathrooms, too, though it was two years before a water main was laid to the site.

The school's quartet sang in programs, and afterwards Mrs. Bethune would describe her aims and needs for the school, then boldly ask for gifts.

"Wouldn't you like to invest in the futures of these little girls?" she would ask. "You may be helping them make a better life for themselves and for their children. They have a stake in America; so have you. Won't you lend them a hand?"

One afternoon, she took her quartet to the big Palmetto Hotel. Only six people showed up to hear them sing, but an elderly gentleman among them dropped a twenty-dollar gold piece into the collection plate. Visiting the school a few days later, he introduced himself as Thomas White. When he saw the school's wheezing old sewing machine, he promised to send out a brand new one. It turned out that he was president of the White Sewing Machine Company. He also gave the school two hundred dollars. "I believe you are on the right track," he said, and backed up his belief with frequent contributions for many years.

Meanwhile, Albertus tried a succession of jobs, but the marriage became less and less meaningful. He returned in 1906 to his old home in Wedgefield, South Carolina, where he died ten years later. Little Albert was sent to boarding school; later he went on to graduate from Morehouse College.

When the roof went up on Faith Hall, Mrs. Bethune called a meeting. "We won't have school today," she announced. "We are moving into our new building."

"But there aren't any floors yet," said one youngster.

"And the plaster hasn't been put on the walls," added another.

"Never mind. We are going in. We will have more room, and it will be more convenient to do some of the work."

The following year, 1908, Mrs. Bethune accepted a few boys as students, expanded her faculty, and changed the name to Daytona Educational and Industrial Training School.

The famous Booker T. Washington arrived one day during the same year to look over the still struggling school. The founder of Tuskegee Institute in Alabama, he, too, knew what it was like to overcome near-impossible odds. As he gazed around crowded Faith Hall, filled with youngsters in secondhand clothing, using makeshift equipment, his face grew sober.

"You have set yourself a difficult task, Mrs. Bethune," he said softly. Then, glancing through a window, he saw half a dozen pigs wallowing in their pens. His face brightened.

"Ah! You have pigs!" he exclaimed. "I am glad you have pigs. There's nothing to compare with pigs as a mortgage lifter; you can exchange them for nearly anything you need. Mrs. Bethune, it will be a hard struggle, but I believe you will make it!"

Reports from the Daytona Institute began to interest persons in both the North and the South. Opportunities for Mrs. Bethune to speak increased, and new funds began to trickle in. South Carolina State College invited Mrs. Bethune to receive an honorary degree; for the occasion, she consented to buy a new dress and hat. During the years to come, she was to receive nine other honorary degrees, including one from all-white Rollins College in Florida in 1949. The Rollins degree was the first honorary degree ever given a black person by a white southern college.

In Daytona, she expanded her activities to organize evening study clubs for women, Sunday school classes and recreation projects in the turpentine camps, and activities for the young boys in the neighborhood. In 1911, the refusal of the city hospital to accept one of her students for an emergency operation led her to purchase a little cottage and set up her own two-bed hospital. It grew within five years into a real hospital with twenty-six beds. Twenty years later, the Daytona city hospital was integrated, and the McLeod hospital building became a teacher training laboratory.

In the early twentieth century, as blacks increasingly asserted the rights guaranteed to them under the Fourteenth and Fifteenth Amendments, they experienced different forms of intimidation. The Ku Klux Klan, formally dissolved before the turn of the century, was reorganized in 1915. Daytona Beach had its own unit. When Mrs. Bethune began holding classes in citizenship and civil rights, just before election time, the Klan decided to take action. One night, a group of hooded riders appeared in the school yard, one of them carrying a burning cross. The head of the group started toward the porch. Suddenly, all the lights in the school came on, and voices of children singing hymns quavered on the night air. In all her dignity, Mrs. Bethune advanced to the edge of the porch.

"We've come to warn you, Mary Bethune," shouted the leader. "Shut down your civics class or we'll burn your school to the ground."

Anger made Mrs. Bethune's voice shake, but she

leaned over and shook her finger at the "ghosts."

"Then I'll build it back, again and again and again." Her strong response came from her faith that heaven would support her school, no matter what happened. She repeated her determination to keep the school going, and then she led the choir of voices in song:

> Blest be the tie that binds
> Our hearts in Christian love . . .

Slowly the men turned away, taking with them the burning cross. The next day, Mrs. Bethune led nearly two hundred black voters to the polls.

By 1923 Mrs. Bethune came to realize that the future of her school was too dependent on one person, herself. After thorough investigation, the board of trustees approved a merger with a boys' school in Jacksonville. The result was Bethune-Cookman Institute, which prospered and grew into the accredited four-year Bethune-Cookman College of today. Mrs. Bethune remained president until 1947; then she became president emeritus.

After the merger, Mrs. Bethune's school no longer depended so heavily on her fund-raising activity. Many persons would have been content to rest, having accomplished so much. But wider fields of service beckoned, and Mary Bethune's vision, energy, and deep faith prodded her on. She later attributed all her achievements to her Christian faith. In an article in *Christian Century* in 1952, she said,

> This power of faith which is my spiritual strength is so infinitely a part of my mental and emotional life that I find integration and harmony ever within me. . . . I always tell my

young people: Walk proudly in the light. Faith ought not to be a puny thing. If we believe, we should believe like giants. I wish this blessing for my students and for American youth everywhere: May God give you not peace, but glory!

Her activities outside her school included writing a weekly column in the Pittsburgh *Courier* and the Chicago *Defender*. She also served as a lay delegate to the General Conference of the Methodist Church. In 1931, she was named to a list of fifty outstanding American women. Four years later, intent on enlarging opportunities for black women, Mrs. Bethune founded the National Council of Negro Women. It included all of the black women's organizations, and it soon had a membership of eight hundred thousand.

The Great Depression of the early 1930s resulted in widespread unemployment, especially among black youths. When Franklin D. Roosevelt became president in 1933, he set up a National Youth Administration to give young people jobs. He named Mrs. Bethune head of the Negro division. Through her work, hundreds of thousands of young people were given jobs or helped to continue their education. Mothers were trained in vocational projects and introduced to modern standards of health and child care. Later Mrs. Bethune was named Director of Minority Affairs for the N.Y.A. It was the first time a black woman had been the head of a government agency.

In 1941, the year the United States entered World War II, Mrs. Bethune became Assistant Director of the Women's Army Corps, helping to recruit black women into the army. President Roosevelt came to respect her abilities and to depend on her advice. She and Mrs.

Roosevelt became close friends, and their friendship continued until Mrs. Bethune's death.

"I like Mary McLeod Bethune," the president often said. "Her feet are always on plowed ground."

Mary Bethune met racial discrimination often throughout her career. But she was able to translate her spiritual faith into a forgiving spirit as she fought for civil rights. She said,

> I meet discrimination with great pity. I feel pity in my heart for those who inflict injustice and unhappiness upon me. Sorrow comes over me because of the smallness of their souls, their failure to measure up to the Christ spirit, their blindness to what brotherhood means. . . . My heart has been touched more with pity than with resentment, and this has kept me from growing bitter.

The 1949 convention of the National Council of Negro Women had as its theme "World Citizenship through Human Understanding." Hopes instilled by the founding of the United Nations (for which Mrs. Bethune had been an official consultant) were still high. At the 1949 convention, Mrs. Bethune was stepping down as president of the council. A host of distinguished guests, including President Harry Truman, came to honor her. Her address was broadcast worldwide over Voice of America radio.

White-haired, and clothed in a long black velvet dress, Mrs. Bethune addressed the audience in her resonant voice. "I am filled with reverent awe that faith and hard work could build so much from the vision of a child toiling in the cotton field," she said. "Let us not be too impatient at the seemingly slow process we are now making toward the goal of world peace."

When she finished the address, cheers filled the hall. Most of those present knew how much she had endured, how hard had been the journey. Some of them recalled a difficult experience she had undergone during the war years. In February of 1943, the chairman of the House Committee on Un-American Activities had accused her of being a Communist. Quickly the American press had come to her defense. And a representative from New York issued this statement:

> . . . I have been a supporter of the Committee from the beginning . . . however, in view of the facts of this woman's life, and to salve my own conscience, . . . I repeat the thought that her type of work is, in my opinion, the most effective antidote against Communistic penetration among the Negroes.

Mrs. Bethune also issued a statement in her own defense, and eventually the Committee's chief investigator protested that he had never claimed she was a Communist, only that she had been on some committees with Communists. The uproar died down. Unfortunately, in the summer of 1971 similar accusations were again brought up in the nation's capital. But several congressmen immediately leapt to their feet to clear once more the good name of Mary McLeod Bethune. No further objections were raised to allowing the Council of Negro Women to collect donations for the Bethune Memorial in Washington, D.C.'s Lincoln Park. The memorial is a sculpture by Robert Berk, portraying Mrs. Bethune, a scroll in her hand, passing on her legacy of love to the children of the future.

In spite of increasing physical infirmities in the

1950s, Mrs. Bethune continued to make speeches and accept awards. Much of her time, however, was spent in her home on the Bethune-Cookman campus. There she received distinguished visitors, talked with students, and viewed with justifiable pride the school of her dream, now grown to a thirty-six-acre campus with nineteen buildings, valued at two million dollars. And it had all started with one dollar and fifty cents!

She was sitting in her rocking chair on her front porch one day in May, 1954, when news came that the Supreme Court had struck down segregation in public schools. She sprang from her chair, new strength suddenly given to her almost eighty-year-old limbs.

*The Bethune Memorial statue in Washington, D.C.*

"The Lord be praised!" she shouted. "Hallelujah!"
That night she wrote in her column for the Chicago *Defender*:

> The wise judges of the high bench saw, without difference of opinion . . . that America needs to provide, for itself and for the Negro, equality in fundamental education. . . . We are on our way. But there are frontiers which we must conquer, pushing our claims further. We must gain full equality in education, full equality in the franchise, full equality in economic opportunity, and full equality in the religious abundance of life.

One year later, on May 18, 1955, Mary McLeod Bethune died. To members of her race, in her Last Will and Testament, she bequeathed the principles and policies in which she had firmly believed:

> *I leave you love* . . . . Loving your neighbor means being interracial, interreligious and international.
>
> *I leave you hope* . . . . Tomorrow, a new Negro, unhindered by race taboos and shackles, will benefit from this striving and struggling.
>
> *I leave you a thirst for education.* More and more, Negroes are taking full advantage of hard-won opportunities for learning. . . .
>
> *I leave you faith* . . . . Faith in God is the greatest power, but great faith too is faith in oneself. . . .
>
> *I leave you racial dignity* . . . . As a race we have given something to the world, and for this we are proud and fully conscious of our place in the total picture of mankind's development.
>
> *I leave you a desire to live harmoniously with*

*your fellow men* . . . . We are a minority . . . living side by side with a white majority. . . . We must learn to deal with people positively and on an individual basis.

*I leave you finally a responsibility to our young people.* Our children must never lose their zeal for building a better world. . . .

# Other Outstanding Women

In addition to the six women featured in this book, there are many hundreds more who have contributed greatly to the field of education. Although it is impossible to discuss them all, here are a few more of education's foremost women.

CATHARINE BEECHER (1800-1878) was an early supporter of education for women. She was the eldest child in a famous American family: Her father and a brother were well-known Protestant ministers, and one of her sisters was Harriet Beecher Stowe, who wrote the antislavery book *Uncle Tom's Cabin*. When she was in her early twenties, Catharine became engaged, but her fiancé was killed shortly afterward. She then turned to teaching, and in 1823 she opened a girls' school with her sister Mary. Four years later it became the Hartford Female Seminary and soon gained a national reputation. In her school, Catharine stressed the importance of home economics, teacher training, and physical exercise. In the 1840s Catharine turned her attention to the western frontier and began working for the education of the large numbers of children who were growing up there without schools. She sent many trained school teachers to the Midwest and also helped open several schools. Although none of the western schools Catharine founded survive today, they were an important influence on education in the Midwestern states.

SUSAN ELIZABETH BLOW (1843-1916) was the founder of the first public school kindergarten in the United States. She discovered the kindergarten work of Friedrich Froebel while traveling in Germany in the 1870s, and she was quickly converted to Froebel's ideas. Returning to her home in St. Louis, Missouri, she she opened a kindergarten in the public schools there in 1873. Unlike earlier American kindergartens, this one was available to all children without payment of a fee. As a result of Susan's influence, by 1880 all the public schools in the St. Louis system had their own kindergartens. That city's system became a model for public schools all over the country. To keep kindergartens running according to Froebel's plan, Susan translated Froebel's book of songs and games, called *Mother Play,* from German to English. By nature Susan had very intense feelings and convictions, and she always held firmly to Froebel's teaching practices and kindergarten philosophy. Later, in the 1900s, other kindergarten teachers began to turn from Froebel and bring kindergartens in line with newer educational ideas. Susan Blow's refusal to adopt anything but Froebel's methods kept her involved in educational debate for the rest of her life.

SARAH FULLER (1836-1927) was a pioneer in the education of the deaf. However, she began her career in a fairly ordinary manner, teaching at a regular school in Boston for fourteen years. But then she took a new direction, one that led her to have a lasting influence on educational ideas. A public school for deaf-mute children was opened in Boston in 1869, and Sarah was asked to be one of the two teachers. At first there were only ten children, but within five years there were sixty-three students. Sarah was named principal of the school (called the Horace Mann School for the Deaf), a position she held for forty-one years. One of her important contributions was showing that deaf children did not have to live at school, but that they could be "day" students just like other children. Previously, schools for the deaf had been primarily boarding schools. Also, Sarah began to teach deaf children to speak, rather than just to use sign language. Up to this time, people had assumed that the deaf could not learn to talk. Another concept that she introduced was that deaf children should begin their education at as early an age as possible. All of these important ideas are still accepted and followed today in this area of education.

LUCY LANEY (1854-1933), whose father was born a slave early in the nineteenth century, was responsible for the education of hundreds of black children of the southern United States. After graduating from Atlanta University in 1873, Lucy taught in various Georgia public schools until 1885. Then she opened a private school for black children in Augusta, Georgia. At first she had only 5 students, but the school was so successful that by the end of the second year she had 234 students. Eventually the Haines Institute (named for one of the school's financial supporters) expanded to cover a city block. By World War I it had nine hundred students and more than thirty teachers. One of Lucy's important gifts was her ability to see beyond the thinking of her day. She emphasized a liberal arts curriculum at a time when vocational training was considered the right kind of education for black people. She inspired her students to enter good colleges and become qualified teachers at a time when the state of Georgia did not even have high schools for black children. After Lucy's death in 1933, the Haines Institute declined, partly because of the Depression of the 1930s, and it finally closed in 1949. Today the site of the school is occupied by the Lucy C. Laney High School.

ALICE FREEMAN PALMER (1855-1902) was an American educator who spent her life working for better education for women. She was named president of Wellesley College, a women's college in Massachusetts, at the age of twenty-seven, thus becoming one of the youngest college presidents in history. Prior to that, she had graduated from the University of Michigan, had served as a high school teacher and principal, and had been head of the history department at Wellesley. Active and dynamic, Alice Freeman established many new policies for Wellesley, and the impact of those policies is still being felt today. While president of the college, she helped found the American Association of University Women, an organization dedicated to promoting women's educational interests. Although she resigned her post in 1887, when she married George Herbert Palmer, she remained influential and active for the rest of her life. She served on the Wellesley board of trustees, on the Massachusetts State Board of Education, and on many important committees.

ELIZABETH PALMER PEABODY (1804-1894) is best known as the founder of the first kindergarten in the United States. Her interest in early childhood education probably came from her mother, who conducted a private school at which Elizabeth was educated. Elizabeth began her educational career before she was twenty years old, teaching first at her mother's school and later at a school she and her sister Mary opened near Boston. She continued teaching until 1834, when she became assistant to Bronson Alcott, a transcendentalist philosopher, in a new school he had opened. Elizabeth's scholarly interests and lively mind led her to friendship with many of the Transcendentalists. Transcendentalism was a nineteenth century philosophy that emphasized, among other ideas, the importance of individual thinking and reasoning. In 1834 Elizabeth gave up teaching and opened a bookstore, where many of the Transcendentalists gathered for discussions. She began publishing writings of many of these philosophers, thus becoming the first woman publisher in the United States. Her bookstore closed in 1850, and Elizabeth went back to education, taking up teaching again and also writing several books and articles on education. Then in 1859 she learned about Friedrich Froebel's kindergarten movement in Germany. The next year she started her own kindergarten in Boston, and it soon attracted national attention. She spent much time from then on promoting this new educational idea, and she saw it gain widespread acceptance over the next thirty years.

MARIA SANFORD (1836-1920) began her forty-year educational career as professor of history at Swarthmore College in Pennsylvania. After ten years at Swarthmore, during which time she also gave many public lectures on moral and social topics, Maria accepted a position at the newly formed University of Minnesota. She served there as professor of rhetoric and elocution until her retirement in 1909, at the age of seventy-two. At the university, Maria Sanford became known as an inspiring teacher and was very popular with her students. She introduced them to poetry and art, which were her own favorite subjects. She continued her public addresses, traveling throughout the country and lecturing on the arts, public affairs, and woman suffrage. Her audiences also liked to hear her read her favorite poems. Maria Sanford in her later years lived in great poverty in order to pay back a debt resulting from an unwise investment. She succeeded in repaying the entire amount shortly before her death. In 1958 the state of Minnesota placed a statue of Maria Sanford in Statuary Hall at the Capitol in Washington, D.C., as a tribute to her educational work.

MARTHA CAREY THOMAS (1857-1935) was a prominent educator who was president of Bryn Mawr College in Pennsylvania for more than twenty-five years. Well-educated, especially for a woman of her time, Carey received her Ph.D. from the University of Zurich in Switzerland. She was the first foreigner and the first woman to do so. Even before Bryn Mawr College opened, Carey was appointed dean and professor of English; ten years later she was named the college's president, a position she held until her retirement in 1922. During her presidency, she worked for strict entrance requirements and high standards of scholarship among the students. She organized a graduate school at Bryn Mawr, the first one connected with any women's college. Also, she established a college preparatory school for girls. Carey Thomas was a leader of the group of women who forced Johns Hopkins medical school to admit women students. These women gave a large sum of money to help open the school, making the admission of women a condition of the gift. Among her many other activities, Carey worked diligently for woman suffrage.

MARY WOOLLEY (1863-1947) was an outstanding educator who was also an active supporter of world peace. Educated at Brown University in Rhode Island, Mary was the first woman to receive a bachelor's degree from that school. After receiving a master's from Brown, Mary began teaching at Wellesley College in 1895 and four years later was promoted to full professor. In 1901, she became the president of Mount Holyoke College. One of her major concerns at Mount Holyoke was increasing academic quality. She hired more qualified faculty members, enlarged the college's graduate school program, and increased the number of student electives. Mary was active in a number of social causes, including better education for women and woman suffrage. She was a member of the American Association of University Women and served as its president for several years. Outside the college she worked most diligently for the cause of world peace. In 1932 she was a United States delegate to an arms reduction conference in Geneva, Switzerland, becoming the first woman to represent the country at an important international conference. She retired from Mount Holyoke in 1937, the one-hundredth year of the existence of the college, when she was seventy-four years old.

# Suggested Reading

Bluemel, Elinor. *Colorado Woman of the Century.* Colorado Press, 1959.
An account of Dr. Sabin's career in public health, after she had supposedly retired from active work.

Bolton, Sarah K. *Lives of Girls Who Became Famous.* Crowell, 1949.
Brief, accurate, and interesting sketches of twenty-two women, including Mary Lyon.

Byers, Tracy. *The Sunday Lady of Possum Trot.* Putnam, 1932.
Many amusing incidents fill the pages of this readable account of Miss Berry and her mountain children.

Daughtery, Sonia. *Ten Brave Women.* Lippincott, 1953.
Biographies of ten American women, including Mary Lyon, who helped shape the country's history.

Embree, Edwin R. *Thirteen Against the Odds.* Viking, 1946.
Biographies of Mary McLeod Bethune and twelve others who accomplished their goals against seemingly impossible odds.

Fleming, Alice. *Great Women Teachers.* Lippincott, 1965.
The life stories of Emma Willard, Mary Lyon, Martha Berry, Mary McLeod Bethune, and other women important in the history of education.

Gilchrist, B. Bradford. *The Life of Mary Lyon.* Houghton Mifflin, 1929.
A detailed portrait of Mary Lyon based on college records and interviews with people who know her personally.

Hartley, Lucie K. *Maria Sanford: Pioneer Professor.* Dillon, 1977.
The story of Maria Sanford's long struggle for acceptance among educators as a professional equal. Her warm personality and eccentric lifestyle make for a lively children's biography.

Holt, Rackham. *Mary McLeod Bethune.* Doubleday, 1964.
Comprehensive and exciting account of Mary McLeod Bethune's life, with many illustrations.

Kane, Harnett T., with Henry, Inez. *Miracle in the Mountains.* Doubleday, 1956.
Inez Henry was Martha Berry's secretary for many years, and many personal memories lend spice to this book.

Lutz, Alma. *Emma Willard, Daughter of Democracy.* Houghton Mifflin, 1929.
This account of Emma Willard's life includes a helpful chronology as well as many illustrations and an excellent bibliography.

Myers, Elizabeth P. *Angel of Appalachia.* Messner, 1968.
Written for readers twelve years and up, this book describes Miss Berry's accomplishments and her strong ambition and determination.

Nathan, Dorothy. *Women of Courage.* Random House, 1964.
Mary McLeod Bethune is one of the five well-known women included in this Landmark book.

Peare, Catherine O. *Mary McLeod Bethune.* Vanguard, 1957.
Readable, fairly brief account of Mary McLeod Bethune's trials and triumphs. A foreword by Mrs. Bethune is included.

Phelan, Mary Kay. *Probing the Unknown.* Crowell, 1969.
Simply written and very interesting biography of Dr. Florence Sabin. It focuses primarily on her work as teacher and researcher.

Mary Wyche Burgess, a former newspaper reporter, has published articles and stories in many publications, including the *South Carolina Magazine, Jack and Jill,* and *Church Herald. Contributions of Women: Education* is her first published book.

Mrs. Burgess graduated from Randolph-Macon Woman's College in Virginia in the 1930s. She returned to school many years later, to earn in 1970 a master's degree in clinical psychology at Furman University in Greenville, South Carolina. She and her husband are residents of Greenville, where Mrs. Burgess is also a violinist with the Greenville Symphony.